DATE DUE

TI   S

Propaganda, Inc.

SELLING AMERICA'S CULTURE TO THE WORLD

NANCY SNOW

Foreword by Herbert I. Schiller
Introduction by Michael Parenti

Series editors Greg Ruggiero and Stuart Sahulka

SEVEN STORIES PRESS / New York

Copyright © 1998 by Nancy Snow

Library of Congress Cataloging-in-Publication Data

Snow, Nancy.
    Propaganda, Inc.: selling America's culture to the world/Nancy Snow .
    p.   cm. —(The Open Media Pamphlet Series)
    ISBN 1-888363-74-6 (pbk.)
    1.United States Information Agency 2.Propaganda, American. 3. United States-Cultrual policy. 4.United States—Relations—Foreign countries.5. Corporate profits—United States. I. Title. II. Series.
E840.2.S6 1998
353.1'3274'0973—dc21   97-52614
                            CIP

Book design by Cindy LaBreacht

9 8 7 6 5 4 3 2 1

Printed in the U.S.A.

FOREWORD

by Herbert I. Schiller

One of the unique talents of American capitalism has been its mastery of salesmanship. This should not be surprising given that marketing has been an indispensable and pervasive feature of the economy since at least the Civil War.

Still, selling a deeply flawed economic system to the people with the same enthusiasm and success devoted to advertising a bar of soap is a challenging assignment. Just as dentifrices and deodorants are extolled as matchless and wondrous, capitalism receives equally rapturous promotion, beginning in children's primers and continuing through succeeding educational and cultural channels across the social order.

One of the tricks of effective advertising is to identify the product with a highly desirable quality that has widespread appeal. A certain toothpaste, for instance, claims to offer a feeling of freshness. In selling the private ownership system to the public, this first principle of hucksterism has been applied with remarkable effectiveness.

In a nation whose origins began with an anti-colonial revolution, freedom and liberty are powerful words. Fully aware of this, generations of systemic hucksters have appropriated these words on behalf of profits and class-dominated governance. This has been the national experience since the First World War.

This cataclysmic event, along with its profound effects on the distribution of world power, has transformed and exponentially increased American propaganda—salesmanship for political goals—domestically and globally.

It ushered in an era of far-reaching American power—economically, politically, and culturally—which produced a giant global shift in influence from the old, worn-out European empires, to the new financial-cultural domain being created by American capital.

To make the emerging American system of domination palatable at home and acceptable abroad to nations which had struggled for centuries against colonialism, a new dimension of propaganda was a necessity.

As Dr. Snow perceptively points out in her text, two overriding objectives comprised the agenda for U.S. propaganda in the postwar period: the defense of the existing capitalist world against threatened social change—socialism in Western Europe and elsewhere—and the capture of the ex-colonial world for private enterprise and foreign capital.

Anti-communism was the instrument that served both objectives as well as the means of gaining domestic support, or at least toleration, for American global interventions and takeovers. Anti-communism turned attention away from pressing problems at home and abroad by focusing hysterically on fabricated external threats. At the same time, it enabled a continually expanding U.S. world presence to be explained as offering protection against communism.

For nearly half a century, the United States Information Agency (USIA) waged ideological war against communism in its worldwide broadcasts. Using the rhetoric of freedom and liberty—the CIA-operated stations in Europe were named Radio Free Europe and Radio Liberty—American propaganda dwelled on the ominous and imminent threat of communism, while U.S. corporations moved into one global space after another.

The influence of the USIA in this period cannot be over-exaggerated. Certainly, the commercial flood of U.S. cultural products that engulfed the world in the last fifty years—movies, TV programs, recordings, publications, student exchanges, theme parks, data bases *et al*—was, by far, the most important means in transmitting ideology, anti-communism and American socio-economic institutions. Yet the USIA did its bit to target those government bureaucrats, intellectuals, local managers, etc., who may have disdained U.S. popular culture.

Once the Soviet system collapsed, however, the propaganda war took a new turn. Again, Dr. Snow is right on target as she charts the shift in the USIA's efforts, away from anti-communism to full devotion to U.S. corporate initiatives, to extend the latter's influence in what Wall Street designated as "emerging market" states, mostly former colonial territories.

Snow makes amply clear that, in this latest propaganda campaign, the use of student and academic exchange programs, and the Agency's mandate to work for mutual understanding between nations, have been perverted into crass missions to assist American companies in finding profitable business overseas.

Yet propaganda has its limits. Reality, at some point, always intrudes. As this is written, people in many Southeast Asian countries are discovering that the bitter truths about the much touted capitalism and its far-flung network of control, cannot indefinitely be made acceptable by propaganda. Despite the powerful transmitters at the disposal of capital, the harsh features of a market organized society and its inherent connection to inequality sooner or later will be recognized and resisted.

Dr. Snow, in this essay, makes a contribution to this end.

Herbert I. Schiller is the author of *Mass Communications and American Empire; Culture, Inc.: The Corporate Takeover of Public Expression;* and most recently, *Information Inequality.*

INTRODUCTION

by Michael Parenti

For generations, a fundamental function of U.S. foreign policy has been to make certain that the natural resources, markets, labor, and capital of other nations were accessible to U.S. corporate investors on the most favorable terms possible. In 1907, Woodrow Wilson offered this candid observation:

"Since trade ignores national boundaries and the manufacturer insists on having the world as a market, the flag of his nation must follow him, and the doors of the nations which are closed against him must be battered down. Concessions obtained by financiers must be safeguarded by ministers of state, even if the sovereignty of unwilling nations be outraged in the process."

In his 1953 State of the Union message President Dwight Eisenhower observed, "A serious and explicit purpose of our foreign policy [is] the encouragement of a hospitable climate for investment in foreign nations." What no U.S. president has ever explained is: What gives the United States the right to dictate the destinies of other nations, mold their development, and intervene forcibly against them when they dare to mark an independent course?

With unfailing consistency, U.S. intervention has been on the side of the rich and powerful of various nations at the expense of the poor and needy. Rather than strengthening democracies, U.S. leaders have over-thrown numerous democratically elected governments or other populist regimes in dozens of countries—from Chile to Guatemala to Indonesia to Mozambique—whenever these nations give evidence of putting the interests of their people ahead of the interests of multi-national corporate investors.

While claiming that such interventions are needed to safeguard democracy in the world, U.S. leaders have given aid and comfort to dozens of tyrannical regimes that have overthrown reformist democratic governments (as in Chile and Guatemala, for instance) and shown themselves to be faithful acolytes of the transnational corporate investors. In 1993, before the United Nations, President Bill Clinton proclaimed, "Our overriding pur-pose is to expand and strengthen the world's community of market-based democracies." In truth, as Nancy Snow shows in this cogent and revealing pamphlet, the empha-sis has been more on the "market-based" and less on the "democracy."

To the American public and to the world, however, as Snow notes, U.S. policy has been represented in the most glowing—and most deceptive—terms. Peace, pros-perity, and democracy have become coded propaganda terms. "Peace" means U.S. global military domination, a kind of Pax Americana. "Prosperity" means subsidiz-ing the expansion of U.S. corporate interests abroad, at the expense of the U.S. taxpayer and the millions of peo-ple in other nations who might be better served by loyal and independent development. And "democracy," Nancy Snow notes, means a system in which political decisions are made by the transnational and publicly unaccountable corporate interests and their government allies, "not based on a populist or participatory ideal of politics but one in which the public's role is minimized."

Global capitalist hegemony is attained by two means. First, there is the global military apparatus. The U.S. defense budget is at least five times larger than any other country's defense expenditures. U.S. naval, air, and ground forces maintain a police presence around the globe, using hundreds of military bases throughout various regions. U.S. advisors train, equip, and finance military and paramilitary forces in countries on every continent. All this to make the world safe for the transnationals.

The other instrument of U.S. intervention might be called "cultural imperialism," the systematic penetration and dominance of other nations' communication and informational systems, educational institutions, arts, religious organizations, labor unions, elections, consumer habits, and lifestyles. Drawing upon both her personal experience and her scholarly investigation, Nancy Snow offers us a critical picture of one of the key instruments of cultural imperialism, the United States Information Agency (USIA). A benign-sounding unit of government supposedly dedicated to informational and cultural goals, USIA is actually in the business of waging disinformation wars on behalf of the Fortune 500.

Operating as a propaganda unit of a corporate-dominated U.S. foreign policy, USIA ran interference for NAFTA, in Snow's words, "doing nothing to advance the more noble goals of mutual understanding and education," while leaving a trail of broken promises about jobs and prosperity. USIA's efforts on behalf of NAFTA and other such undertakings have brought fantastic jumps in profits for big business, at great cost to the environment, democratic sovereignty, and worker and consumer well-being.

Nancy Snow also deals with the larger issues that go beyond the USIA, especially the way the U.S. political system is dominated and distorted by moneyed interests, transforming democracy into plutocracy, and making a more democratic U.S. foreign policy improbable.

Still, as Snow reminds us, victories can be won when broad-based democratic forces unite and fight back vigorously. A recent example would be the defeat of fast-track legislation in Congress in 1997 in the face of a massive blitz launched by powerful business associations, the White House, and the major media. Snow concludes with a useful and instructive seven-point agenda for a citizen-based diplomacy, pointing out how readers can and should get involved.

In the pages ahead, Nancy Snow shows herself to be a discerning, fair-minded investigator, a skilled writer and researcher, and a socially conscious citizen. No wonder she found herself unable to function within the U.S. propaganda machine. She's too good for Corporate America.

Michael Parenti is the author of *Against Empire; Blackshirts and Reds: Rational Fascism and the Overthrow of Communism;* and the recently published *America Besieged.*

To criticize one's country is to do it a service and pay it a compliment.
— J. William Fulbright, *The Arrogance of Power*

The twentieth century has been characterized by three developments of great political importance: the growth of democracy, the growth of corporate power, and the growth of corporate propaganda as a means of protecting corporate power against democracy.
— Alex Carey, *Taking the Risk Out of Democracy*

Just two blocks from the Mall and the most visited museum in the world, the National Air and Space Museum, are the headquarters of the United States Information Agency (USIA). The USIA receives annual support of about one billion dollars from the American taxpayers but this U.S. government agency is no tourist attraction. In fact, it is unlikely that most Americans would have heard of it. It's one of the best-kept secrets in Washington. This is ironic because the U.S. Information Agency, as the name implies, *is* the information and communication branch of our foreign policy establishment, targeting overseas audiences[1] (U.S. law does not allow Americans to receive USIA information). It's easier abroad to learn about the USIA whose motto is "telling America's story to the world." But don't pack your bags just yet. Take an armchair tour with me.

THE USIA: OUR GOVERNMENT'S "OFFICIAL" PROPAGANDA AGENCY

The USIA is in the export business. It manufactures a favorable point of view about America to foreign audiences, presumably to advance the national interests of the U.S. government. It does this through various means: diplomatic posts known overseas as the U.S. Information Service (USIS), exchange activities such as the Fulbright and International Visitor programs, information programs, and international broadcasting which includes the Voice of America.[2]

The USIA likes to call its particular branch of foreign affairs "public diplomacy," a euphemism for propaganda.[3] The encyclopedia definition for propaganda is "instruments of psychological warfare aimed at influencing the actions of human beings in ways that are compatible with the national-interest objectives of the purveying state."[4] USIA prefers the term public diplomacy to propaganda because it doesn't want the American public to think that its own government engages in psychological warfare and because "propaganda" in the United States is a pejorative term for negative or offensive manipulation, particularly in the political arena.

Propaganda is also thought to characterize primarily the heinous activities of 20th-century totalitarian regimes, like National Socialism or Stalinist communism that used state-sanctioned methods to deliberately distort the truth. Many Americans today view their own government and other professed democracies like the United States generally as tellers of the truth except, of course, in wartime or when trying to win over converts during the cold war.[5] It would surprise many Americans to learn that our own government has a decades-long history of propagandizing its own population and other countries.

THE USIA'S PROTOTYPE: THE CREEL COMMISSION

During the first three years of World War I, the United States remained neutral. On August 19, 1914, President Wilson issued a declaration of neutrality to Congress: "Every man who loves America will act and speak in the true spirit of neutrality, which is the spirit of impartiality and fairness and friendliness to all concerned." He went on to describe the United States as "the one great nation at peace, the one people holding itself ready to play a part of impartial mediation and speak the counsels of peace and accommodation, not as a partisan, but as a friend."[6] Many Americans were decisively pacifistic and even reelected President Wilson to a second term in office on a "Keep America out of the War" ticket. To try to sway American public opinion and to gain sympathy for the Allied cause, the British government set up a secret war propaganda bureau in 1914. The most successful British propaganda technique was to target influential persons and opinion leaders in U.S. government, business, education, and media. As one document put it: "It is better to influence those who can influence others than attempt a direct appeal to the mass of the population."[7]

On April 2, 1917, just six months after Wilson's reelection, he delivered his message of war to Congress: "Neutrality is no longer feasible or desirable where the peace of the world is involved and the freedom of its peoples, and the menace to that peace and freedom lies in the existence of autocratic governments backed by organized force which is controlled by their will, not the will of their people."[8] He made it clear in his message of war that "we have no quarrel with the German people. We have no feeling toward them but one of sympathy and friendship."

The U.S. declared war on Germany four days later. One week later the U.S. government set up its own propaganda organization, the Committee on Public Information (CPI), which would become so successful an operation that it would lead to the eventual establishment of the U.S. Information Agency.

A well-known American journalist, George Creel, who described the CPI as "a plain publicity proposition, a vast enterprise in salesmanship, the world's greatest adventure in advertising," headed the CPI.[9] The Creel Committee had two sections: one domestic, to propagandize the American public against the Germans, and one foreign, which was divided into a foreign press bureau, a wireless and cable service, and the foreign film service. The foreign section soon supervised offices in more than thirty countries.

George Creel and his committee members had to convince the American people that a war some 4,000 miles away was worth fighting. The first transatlantic flight was still two years away and the American soil was not directly threatened. Creel explained the entire propaganda operation in his book, *How We Advertised America: The First Telling of the Amazing Story of the Committee on Public Information that Carried the Gospel of Americanism to Every Corner of the Globe.*[10] Creel estimated that 72 million copies of thirty different booklets about American ideals and the purposes of war were sent across the United States while millions were sent abroad. He organized a group of 75,000 influential speakers, nicknamed the "Four Minute Men" for the average length of their patriotic speeches.[11] These men gave more than one million speeches to 400 million people at home and abroad. Creel's strategy worked to sell war bonds, aid in the recruitment of soldiers, and stir up popular sentiment for war.

Even the new Hollywood film industry helped to exploit a weekly film audience of 80 million. One film, *The Little American*, by the legendary director Cecil B. De Mille, starred child actress Mary Pickford as a young American girl who travels to France to visit her aunt. Along the way, a German submarine torpedoes her ship. The girl survives and witnesses more German atrocities while in France. She supplies information to the French about German positions, is later arrested by the Germans but is rescued before she is due to be executed by firing squad. Other American films, like *The Hun Within*, *The Kaiser*, *The Beast of Burden*, and *The Claws of the Hun*, suggested that the German threat was right on American soil. If the American filmgoers were not sufficiently saturated with nationalistic messages, one of the Four-Minute Men would appear between reel changes to rally more anti-German support.

Edward Bernays, the father of modern public relations, was the Creel Committee's chief for Latin America. He persuaded some of the largest U.S. corporations of the day (Ford, Studebaker, Remington Typewriter, National City Bank, and International Harvester) to open up their Latin-American retail outlets as Creel Committee outposts. "Pamphlets and other publications were distributed to customers, and posters and photographic displays filled windows. Advertising was sometimes given or denied to Latin American papers in accordance with the editorial attitude toward the war."[12]

The Creel Committee successfully merged business with government interests. The Creel approach worked so well that Americans learned to hate German civilians as much if not more than the targeted enemy, the German government. Fitzhugh Green observes in his 1988 account, *American Propaganda Abroad:* "If anyone, even today, questions the domestic impact of CPI, he has only to ask educated Americans why we fought World War I. Inevitably he will hear that it was the 'war to end all wars,' 'save the world for democracy,' and to put down the Kaiser who started it all anyway.... Creel virtually brainwashed the American citizenry."[13]

While the British had first demonstrated to the world the power of wartime propaganda, they abandoned it in peacetime. The United States, led by Bernays, took up the mantle of propaganda campaigns in manufacturing public support for American-style democracy. In *Crystallizing Public Opinion, Engineering Consent,* and *Propaganda,* Bernays argued that American public opinion must be engineered from above by society's few masters, the intelligent minorities, to control the rabble. Bernays described these engineers of consent as "the invisible government ... concentrated in the hands of a few because of the expense of manipulating the social machinery which controls the opinions and habits of the masses."[14]

One of Bernays's first successes was convincing American women that smoking was glamorous and liberating (women's suffrage had been passed in 1920), despite common fears that smoking was associated with prostitution. He did this by hiring models to march in New York's Easter parade in 1929, each holding a lit cigarette and wearing a banner proclaiming it a "torch of liberty." Women made Bernays's client brand, Lucky Strike, an overnight success.[15]

In the 1930s, Bernays worked with corporate America to convince the American people that social movements and worker rights were a threat to American business and, in turn, the American way of life.[16] The business world was reacting to the growing political power of the masses and turned to Bernays to "indoctrinate citizens with the capitalist story" until they were able to play back the story with remarkable fidelity.[17] It was a very successful public relations campaign whose anti-labor and pro-corporate sentiments continue to the present. As of 1995, the United States had more public relations professionals (150,000) than reporters (130,000). Academics like Mark Dowie estimated that about 40 percent of what we consider "news" was generated directly by public relations offices.[18]

THE USIA'S COLD WAR ORIGINS

In June 1942, President Roosevelt coordinated all public information into the Office of War Information (OWI) which set up twenty-six posts overseas known as the U.S. Information Service (USIS). By 1948, the U.S. had passed the Smith-Mundt Act to establish the first peacetime propaganda agency whose purpose was "to promote a better understanding of the United States in other countries, and to increase mutual understanding."[19] With it, Truman initiated his "Campaign of Truth" to direct U.S. propaganda activities against the spread of international communism. By June 1950, Truman's cold war propaganda machine was put to the test as U.S. forces entered South Korea under the United

Nations banner to fight North Korea. The U.S. military was not used to working closely with propagandists who employed psychological warfare tactics to influence rather than kill the enemy.

Fitzhugh Green explains a noteworthy exception to this lack of military faith in "psywar" action in his book, *American Propaganda Abroad.* An American officer who had fought in Korea "recalled how the U.S. artillery fired some leaflet-loaded shells set for high burst over a steep-sloped valley in North Korea. The surrender tracts floated gently down onto the forested ravine. Moments after they landed, one or two Chinese infantrymen appeared from the trees, picked up the papers, and studied them. Sure enough, they started in the direction of the UN command headquarters. The leaflets promised a safe conduct to the rear and good treatment as prisoners of war until peace could be restored. Minutes later, he observed from his artillery post that hundreds of enemy soldiers were striding south. Finally, there appeared to be two or three thousand of them. 'What happened then?' I asked. 'Oh,' he laughed uneasily, 'we reloaded our guns with antipersonnel ammunition and wiped out the whole lot.' 'So you would agree that psywar is effective?' I pursued. 'Why yes, you might say that it can be devastating....'"[20]

Aside from that bloody war account, the USIA's origins were more cold war in emphasis. When the Soviets launched the satellite Sputnik in 1957, the U.S. Advisory Commission on Information responded with a plea for more propaganda, not less. Like President Kennedy's missile-gap theory that justified increased military spending and began the U.S. arms race with the Soviets in the 1960s, a culture gap in the late 1950s would justify increased expenditures in propaganda. "The United States may be a year behind in mass technological education. But it is thirty years behind in competition with communist propaganda...each year sees the communists increase their hours of broadcasting, their production and distribution of books, their motion pictures and cultural exchanges and every other type of propaganda and information activity.... We should start planning to close the gap in this field before it widens further."[21]

In many parts of the world today, and in most dictionaries, propaganda has no inherent negative connotation. It is widely accepted that advertising and public relations employ propagandistic techniques in order to sell merchandise or image. Three important characteristics of propaganda are that (1) it is intentional communication, designed to change the attitudes of the targeted audience; (2) it is advantageous to the persuader in order to further the persuader's cause vis-à-vis an audience (which explains why advertising, public relations, and political campaigns are forms of propaganda); and (3) it is usually one-way information (i.e., a mass media campaign) as opposed to education which is two-way and interactive.[22]

This is why I favor the use of the word "propaganda" over "public diplomacy" to describe the modern operations of the U.S. Information Agency. I consider the USIA a public relations instrument of corporate propaganda which "sells" America's story abroad by integrating business interests with cultural objectives. In the same way that the Creel Commission persuaded the American population during World War I to accept without questioning a total war against Germany and the German people, the USIA utilizes psychological warfare to promote the superiority of American free enterprise, the expansion of

American business interests overseas, and the promotion of the U.S. economy as a model for how other market economies can succeed in the global economy. American commercial interests have come to dominate U.S. foreign policy in general and the USIA in particular although anticommunism remains a small element, as in state-sponsored media operations directed at Cuba and China.

I offer this critique of the corporate domination of the USIA as one who experienced these events firsthand. From 1992-1994, I participated in a federal government program for graduate students called the Presidential Management Intern (PMI) program. The PMI program was initiated by former President Jimmy Carter to attract our nation's best and brightest graduate students to public service through enticing offers of fast-track government management opportunities. My first and only PMI interview was at the United States Information Agency. The USIA was interested in hiring me for several reasons: I was about to receive my Ph.D. in international relations from The American University's School of International Service; I had just defended my doctoral dissertation on "Fulbright Scholars as Cultural Mediators" in which I documented the range of literature on cultural exchange and study abroad; and I was a Fulbright scholar to Germany where I pursued graduate study in political science. Finally, I had accrued several years work experience in the private sector as a cultural exchange specialist.[23]

I worked in the USIA's Bureau of Educational and Cultural Affairs, (the "E Bureau" in government-speak), the purpose of which is to conduct cultural programs which increase mutual understanding between the people of the United States and people of other countries. All E Bureau programs were administered under Public Law 87-256, the

Mutual Educational and Cultural Exchange Act of 1961, best known as the Fulbright-Hays Act. The Fulbright-Hays Act still provides the legislative authority for the Fulbright program and other educational exchange programs like the International Visitor program. The main objective of the Act is to "enable the government of the United States to increase mutual understanding between the people of the United States and the people of other countries...and thus to assist in the development of friendly, sympathetic, and peaceful relations, between the United States and other countries of the world."[24]

While working in the E Bureau, I acted as the USIA contact for the Fulbright program in Germany, Spain, and the former Yugoslavia. Having been a Fulbright recipient, I very much believed in the ideals of educational exchange as illustrated by Senator Fulbright's remarks in *The Price of Empire:* "The one thing that gives me some hope is the ethos that underlies the educational exchange program. That ethos, in sum, is the belief that international relations can be improved, and the danger of war significantly reduced, by producing generations of leaders, who through the experience of educational exchange, will have acquired some feeling and understanding of other peoples' cultures, why they operate as they do, why they think as they do, why they react as they do, and of the differences among these cultures. It is possible, not very probable, but possible that people can find in themselves, through intercultural education, the ways and means of living together in peace."[25]

Fulbright's idealistic sentiment was what made him opposed to housing his namesake educational exchange program in the U.S. Information Agency. He wasn't altogether thrilled about the existence of the USIA in general and even supported a plan by Senator Claiborne Pell in 1987 to dismantle the agency. Had the plan been accepted, the Smithsonian Institution would have become home to American cultural affairs and the Fulbright program (because its emphasis was on education and not propaganda). Public affairs and policy making would return to the State Department and the *Voice of America* would operate like a BBC–style independent organization. The plan never took shape and the USIA undertook a new post–cold war propaganda emphasis on democracy and free markets under the Clinton administration. The Fulbright program in particular and educational exchange in general were to become useful promotional tools for the supremacy of the American economic model and global integration.

By the fall of 1993, as the deal-making over NAFTA marked the halls of Congress, the USIA was quietly building its own NAFTA–inspired trilateral educational system between the U.S., Mexico, and Canada. At a trinational conference on higher education in Vancouver, USIA director Joseph Duffey announced: "Economic integration without a deepening of our educational and cultural dimension poses an unacceptable risk: a collision of values that could well lead to more discord than we would have had without NAFTA."[26]

At the conference, the historically leftist, anti–U.S. National Autonomous University (UNAM) in Mexico City announced for the first time that it was providing 5 million pesos (about $1.6 million) in scholarships for Mexican students and professors to study in the U.S. and Canada. Texas A&M University, which already had agreements with 20 Mexican institutions, announced that it had become the first U.S. university to establish a permanent presence in Mexico. The new university would share floor space in downtown Mexico City with the Texas Chamber of Commerce. Most of the trilateral participants were emphasizing international business in their curriculum. San Diego State and Southwest Community College, with U.S. federal funding, announced the creation of the first U.S.-Mexico undergraduate degree in international business. Participating students would spend two years on an American campus and two years at a Tijuana college. Said Paul Ganster of San Diego State: "This is a logical culmination of those concerned about educating the NAFTA generation. They can be competitive on both sides of the border."[27]

The Fulbright program's educational mission to enhance mutual understanding is increasingly measured against the USIA's propaganda purpose to "explain and support American foreign policy and promote U.S. understanding between the United States and other nations by conducting educational and cultural activities."[28] Jeffrey Gayner, a senior fellow at the conservative Heritage Foundation, argued in a report prepared for the Fulbright program's 50th anniversary that the Fulbright program's emphasis on mutual understanding "neglected the complementary mission of supporting the USIA's mandate to promote American foreign policy."[29] This negligence was tacitly acknowledged by John P. Loiello, Associate Director for Educational and Cultural Affairs at the USIA, in comments to the annual meeting of the Fulbright Association in October 1994. He noted that legislators in Congress "will ask more difficult questions, like how does mutual understanding relate to initiatives on sustainable development, integration in the world economy and U.S. competitiveness."[30] (While working as a presidential management intern in the E Bureau, I considered short-term U.S. foreign economic policy objectives a political intrusion into the independence of this prestigious educational program. The trend continues, however.)

The post–NAFTA conversion of educational exchange was evident most recently during President Clinton's May 1997 state visit to Mexico. The USIA announced a doubling of the U.S.–Mexico Fulbright program, adding about 200 new Mexican and U.S. student scholarships a year. The reason for the Fulbright expansion in Mexico was purely economic, as indicated by a USIS Washington File report: "The expansion of this program will strengthen educational opportunities in both countries and build on the success of NAFTA whereby exports to Mexico are up 37 percent, an all-time high, creating jobs for Americans. Moreover, even during Mexico's financial crisis, the Mexican government maintained its Fulbright contribution, an impressive statement of the value it places on the program."[31] This announcement comes at a time when the overall Fulbright program struggles to maintain its current level of funding. It appears that countries with no geo-economic value are destined for further cuts or complete cut-offs under this free-trade-inspired Fulbright program.

Mutual understanding is a two-way, educationally oriented process that is decidedly nonpropagandistic. It should stand on its own merits, free of commercial tie-ins or short-term foreign policy goals. Unfortunately the USIA has downplayed its worthy ideals about mutual understanding and functions more like a full-time cheerleader for U.S.–led economic and cultural dominance of the global economy. This renewed hucksterism may be characteristic of the passing of the cold war but it raises the ire of other countries, even America's closest allies, which are increasingly critical of U.S. dominance in the political, economic, and cultural sector. As illustrated by *Washington Post* writer William Drozdiak, an October 1997 cover story in the German magazine *Der Spiegel* charged that "the Americans are acting, in the absence of limits put to them by anybody or anything, as if they own a blank check in their 'McWorld.' Strengthened by the end of communism and an economic boom, Washington seems to have abandoned its self-doubts from the Vietnam trauma. America is now the Schwarzenegger of international politics: showing off muscles, obtrusive, intimidating. Never before in modern history has a country dominated the earth so totally as the United States does today. Globalization wears a 'Made in the USA' label."[32]

When 150 countries gathered in Bonn, Germany in October 1997 to craft a global warming treaty, the *Washington Post* reported that the U.S. received almost universal condemnation for not accepting greater responsibility for its production of carbon dioxide and greenhouse gases. "How can the Americans, with around 5 percent of the world's population, go on accounting for a quarter of its greenhouse gases? This flagrant imbalance cannot be allowed to continue," said Klaus Kinkel, Germany's foreign minister.[33]

Other allies are bothered that the U.S. wants to dictate its foreign policy to other countries. After the Denver summit of the world's leading industrial democracies in June 1997, French Prime Minister Lionel Jospin echoed the sentiment of other countries when he said, "We see a certain tendency toward hegemony, which is not necessarily identical with exercising the global responsibilities of a great power, even if it is a friend."[34] When South African President Nelson Mandela was criticized by the United States for visiting Libyan leader Moammar Gadhafi, he rebuffed such criticism: "How can they (the U.S.) have the arrogance to dictate to us where we should go or which countries should be our friends? We cannot accept that a state assumes the role of the world's policeman."[35] It appears that even friendly allies are flexing their muscles now that cold war loyalties have disappeared. This underscores the need for the USIA to reassess its U.S.–first projection of global supremacy.

For some reason, even though the United States celebrates free expression and dissent in the abstract, it is often met with great scorn when it is exercised. As Senator William J. Fulbright writes in his 1966 book, *The Arrogance of Power*, "Intolerance of dissent is a well-noted feature of the American national character."[36] His words are echoed by the Frenchman Alexis de Tocqueville who wrote in *Democracy in America:* "I know of no country in which there is so little independence of mind and real freedom of discussion as in America."[37]

Fulbright believed that lack of independent thinking is especially acute in the federal bureaucracy that has a "congenital inhospitality" to unorthodox ideas. "In most, if not all government agencies, originality, especially at the lower levels, is regarded as a form of insolence or worse."[38]

The PMI program was, ironically enough, designed to bring in fresh blood and new ideas. My academic background in international relations and international communication served me well throughout my two years at the USIA (including a four-month work rotation at the

State Department). I received favorable evaluations of my work, including a commendation by the J. William Fulbright Foreign Scholarship Board, and I was selected to represent the USIA in two cultural exchanges to Japan. The agency often asked me to prepare speeches illustrating USIA's value in a post-cold war era, including the time I prepared quotes about the value of educational and cultural exchange for President Clinton's First Inaugural Address (which he didn't use!).

Just weeks before my PMI program ended in 1994, I was asked to prepare a speech for John P. Loiello, the director of the Bureau of Educational and Cultural Affairs, for a conference on culture and diplomacy. The speech illustrated the USIA's commitment to merging commerce and culture in national security and foreign policy objectives, particularly in the new Bureau of Information, the "I Bureau."

The I Bureau's launching in the fall of 1994 underscored the preeminence of the advocacy and promotion function of the USIA over its educational and cultural mission. The I Bureau's mission is to distribute information to USIS field offices in support of the vital interests of the United States. These vital interests are defined as explaining and advocating American foreign policy through the dissemination of "authoritative texts and expert interpretation"; facilitating the free flow of information, enhancing access to information technology, and promoting respect for intellectual property rights; representing "enduring American values, particularly the U.S. commitment to freedom and equality"; and promoting and supporting democratization, human rights, the rule of law, market economies, and the peaceful resolution of disputes.[39]

I completed my PMI program and received an ami-cable divorce from a bureaucratic career path. My pref-erences for mutual understanding and cultural democracy were clearly at odds with the economic pri-orities and national security objectives of the USIA. My purpose now as an educator and activist is to publicly air what I experienced while working inside the USIA's bureaucracy, to develop a credible critique of a corporate-based diplomacy, and to offer an alternative civil-based diplomacy. When my students finish reading this pam-phlet, they'll recognize the spirit of Fulbright in this reminder: the pursuit of truth, as a form of political action, is inherently disruptive, anti-authoritarian, and dangerous to those content with the way things are. So if you tell the truth, be prepared to remain open to the criticism that always follows.

THE ART OF PROPAGANDA

Propaganda, by definition, must have a target audi-ence. The USIA's audience is determined by the politi-cal ideology of the propagandist. In other words, the USIA targets primarily elite clients from the upper class business and professional echelon who will look to the United States as the world's leader. Clients often par-ticipate in sponsored visits as guests of the United States government, like in the International Visitor Program. These clients are the roughly 10 to 20 percent of the tar-get population with promise or influence potential, rel-atively high education, and who play some role in political and economic decision making. They are mostly journalists/editors, academicians, and entrepreneurs who would benefit from a three-week information tour of the United States.

As a cultural affairs consultant, I have worked with these International Visitors on numerous occasions. Not all of them are predisposed to support the United States and some are actually chosen expressly for their strong anti-American feelings.[40] Nevertheless, millions of U.S. taxpayer dollars have been spent to "host" these visitors, all with the goal of persuading them to support the national interest and foreign policy of the U.S. government.

The USIA targets the educated elite, despite some negative sentiments, because propaganda is thought to be most effective on the small minority of powerful influence peddlers. As Noam Chomsky explains, "One reason that propaganda often works better on the educated than on the uneducated is that educated people read more, so they receive more propaganda. Another is that they have jobs in management, media, and academia, and therefore work in some capacity as agents of the propaganda system—and they believe what the system expects them to believe. By and large, they're part of the privileged elite, and share the interests and perceptions of those in power."[41]

From USIA's perspective, the educated elite are in the best position to design and influence pro-America policy in their respective countries. What about the mass majority, those 80 to 90 percent whom journalist Walter Lippmann calls the "bewildered herd"? They are expected to simply go along with the program and not trouble themselves with political or economic decision making. In his book, *The Phantom Public,* Lippmann said that "the public must be put in its place, so that it may exercise its own powers, but no less and perhaps even more, so that each of us may live free of the trampling and roar of a bewildered herd. Only the insider can make decisions, not because he is inherently a better man but because he is so placed that he can understand and can act. The outsider is necessarily ignorant, usually irrelevant, and often meddlesome."[42]

The USIA uses various media, including overseas radio broadcasts like the Voice of America and its television counterpart Worldnet, to further influence society's insiders. For the most part, the so-called "bewildered herd" isn't expected to pay much attention to these USIA broadcasts and business-as-usual. The herd is seen as the target audience of the commercial mass media through tabloid news, professional sports, and popular television.

THE USIA: FROM COLD WARRIOR TO COMMERCIAL AGENT

Throughout the cold war, the USIA operated Radio Free Europe to communist Eastern Europe and Radio Liberty to the Soviet Union, both of which received credit for helping the U.S. to win the cold war. In the 1980s, the Reagan Administration created Radio/TV Martí to undermine Fidel Castro's government in Cuba and win support from anti-Castro Cubans in Florida. Radio/TV Martí was the first triumph of the Cuban American National Foundation, brainchild of Richard Allen, Reagan's first national security adviser, who envisioned an organization for anti-communist Cuban exiles that would be for Cuba what the American-Israel Political Action Committee (AIPAC) was for Israel.

Today Radio/TV Martí is much maligned, and the USIA's Office of Cuba Broadcasting is overly politicized with supporters of the Cuban-American National Foundation (CANF) and its controversial founder, the late

Jorge Mas Canosa, who chaired the the USIA's Advisory Board for Cuba Broadcasting. Canosa was able to use his bullying charisma and his organization's clout to secure millions of dollars in annual funding for Radio Martí and its TV cousin, despite internal reports that acknowledged TV Martí "achieves virtually no reception or impact within the greater Havana area due to heavy jamming."[43] A 1997 article by Wayne Smith of the Center for International Policy (and former chief of the U.S. Interests Section in Havana) revealed that TV Martí's signal, which comes from a balloon high above the Florida Keys, uses the same transmission signal that the U.S. government operates to track incoming drug flights. When TV Martí's transmission goes on, the drug smuggling radar goes off.[44] The evidence is clear that Radio/TV Martí is a cold war weapon controlled by powerful special interests that no government official will challenge. Evidence aside, in 1997 the Office of Cuba Broadcasting was relocated to Miami, Florida at taxpayer expense, to the irritation of Castro and to the delight of CANF supporters.

The newest broadcasting arm of the USIA is Radio Free Asia. Patterned after Radio Free Europe, RFA began broadcasting to China in September 1996 and now airs programs for North Korea, Tibet, Vietnam, Laos, and Burma. The mission of Radio Free Asia is to broadcast truthful information to countries where governments censor information and outright ban freedom of the press. Congressional debate over this new government-broadcasting venture was contentious. Opponents argued that the Voice of America was already broadcasting to the same countries, had built up a huge audience and had brand-name credibility. RFA proponents supported an operation that would broadcast entirely in the native language of the targeted countries and employ regular journalists, area specialists, and "information specialists" whose goal is to destabilize government control over the population. In other words, the RFA concept is much like Radio/TV Martí; it functions primarily as a propaganda operation, which disturbs all who support a free and open model of information exchange. In a recent *Christian Science Monitor* editorial, Pat Holt, former Chief of Staff to the Senate Foreign Relations Committee, wrote that "targeted propaganda broadcasts, such as Radio Martí to Cuba and Radio Free Asia to China, should be ended."[45] Her opinion is not shared by the Senate Foreign Relations Committee chairman, Senator Jesse Helms (R-NC), who enjoys bipartisan support for the preservation of these so-called "Freedom Radios" that target overseas political elites and opinion-leaders.

The crucial issue remains: whether or not the United States government should continue to export its benign-sounding but essentially undemocratic "market democracy" through propaganda vehicles like international broadcasting and cultural exchange programs.

Throughout the cold war, the USIA's professed messianic mission was to counter Soviet propaganda and win the battle for men's minds by "telling America's story abroad," the motto of the USIA which remains today embossed at the entrance of its Washington headquarters. Since the U.S. "won" its psychological warfare with Soviet communism, the USIA has shifted gears to new Clinton foreign policy objectives of commercial engagement and expanding markets overseas.

The USIA launched its post-cold war capitalistic campaign in the mid-1980s by funding the National Endowment for Democracy (NED) and the Center for International Enterprise (CIPE). NED and CIPE were preceded by President Ronald Reagan's Project Democracy and Project Truth campaigns which claimed to spread the ideals of democracy at the height of U.S. military aid spending to Latin America. Project Democracy, like Project Truth, was an effort to combat Soviet propaganda campaigns, and included symposia to help build "positive attitudes toward democracy" among third-world dictators.[46]

Project Democracy and its offspring, the National Endowment for Democracy, were efforts that began with Reagan's June 1982 address to the British Parliament in which he called for a new war of ideas and values with the Soviet Union and its allies. In many respects, Reagan's British Parliament address was the first sign of a shift in U.S. policy from the policy of containment to a policy of advocacy for democracy and free markets. Some members of Congressional oversight committees were initially skeptical of the USIA's new effort to propagandize democracy, particularly when it was learned that former CIA director William Casey attended a planning meeting for the Project Democracy initiative. The academic community weighed in with its resistance as well. "If the United States wants to propagate democracy, it should do it by example," said Professor Stanley Hoffmann of Harvard University. Peter Magrath, former president of the University of Minnesota, called Project Democracy "propaganda and hard-sell," and as a means for promoting democracy, "hard-sell doesn't work."[47] Hampshire College president Adele Simmons expressed concern that the project's tone was culturally imperialistic and "suggests that our way is better than their way."[48]

Most concerns centered on the effect that this new

propaganda campaign would have on the Fulbright program. The Fulbright program, in the eyes of scholars and participants, espoused democracy by example instead of indoctrination. In response to these democracy advocacy campaigns, Congress passed the Pell amendment, named for Senator Claiborne Pell (D-RI), which called for a doubling of U.S. government exchanges by 1986 to $135 million, a goal that in principle was a top USIA priority but which was never met in reality.

Ever since the passage of NAFTA in 1993 and with U.S.–Soviet tensions no longer a viable rationale, the USIA has embraced trade and economics as its primary mission. At the start of the Clinton administration, former national security adviser Anthony Lake announced a new rationale for U.S. foreign policy: "Throughout the cold war, we contained a global threat to market democracies. Now we should seek to enlarge their reach, particularly in places of special significance to us. The successor to a doctrine of containment must be a strategy of enlargement, the enlargement of the world's free community of market democracies."[49]

The USIA carries out the policies of our first post–cold war president through the Clinton Doctrine, which places U.S. competitiveness and integration of the world economy at the heart of our foreign policy. "One of the most important areas for enhanced agency activity is that of business, trade, and economics. More and more, we are teaching others not only about the principles of free markets but the very mechanisms that make free markets and open trade possible," USIA Director Joseph Duffey told a Senate Foreign Relations subcommittee in 1993.[50] That economic message became the agency's *raison d'être* in the post-Soviet environment. In a USIA/VOA editorial, then-

Senator Howell Heflin (D-AL) asserted that the USIA continues to serve a "vital purpose of telling America's story to the rest of the world. These (USIA) programs not only serve our national security interests, they also provide direct economic benefits and foster a climate where American business can develop overseas markets. These markets produce jobs and provide wages for American workers and workers in the host country."[51]

If there ever were a White Paper on the intersection of public diplomacy with U.S. business and trade interests, it appeared in a publication distributed to all USIA employees worldwide. In the May 1994 issue of "News and Views," a publication of the USIA's American Federation of Government Employees, Local 1812, E Bureau's Rhonda Boris announced a restructuring of the USIA mission for 1995 that would convert 150 binational centers and 132 USIS American centers overseas in ways that "activate the link between U.S. public diplomacy and trade promotion and support the new U.S. foreign policy of penetrating the Department of Commerce–designated 'Big Emerging Markets.'"[52] The USIA was developing a "new synergy between public diplomacy and trade promotion in the information age," which had the potential to "become the growth industry for the USIA. The vision is ours to embrace."[53]

This article, along with hundreds of supporting VOA editorials, signifies an agency that acts first and foremost for the promotion of American business interests overseas. The USIA's operation as a mini–Commerce Department makes for duplication of government services in a post–big government era of downsizing and budget cuts. But the USIA aims to further synergize the public/private partnership between corporate America and foreign affairs.

The USIA Strategic Plan for 1997-2003 includes national security, democracy, law enforcement, and economic prosperity as vital agency goals. The overlapped goals of economic and national security lead to agency functions that include NATO expansion (which is expected to create a boom market for U.S. arms manufacturers);[54] anticrime and antiterrorism information programs in cooperation with the Department of Justice and FBI; collaboration with the Drug Enforcement Administration to create public affairs programming; and protection of intellectual property rights.

The USIA uses "national security" and "democracy" interchangeably with "free enterprise" and "the free market."[55] Economic prosperity is defined as "expand exports, open markets, assist American business, and foster sustainable economic growth."[56] "Democracy" means a system in which business interests and their government allies make political decisions that run the free enterprise system of private profit and public subsidy, i.e. the military-industrial complex. The people are permitted to endorse the decisions of their leaders by voting occasionally, but otherwise are not expected to meddle in the affairs of the private/public partnership. This neoliberal model of market democracy is not based on a participatory ideal of politics but on one in which the public's role is minimized, and transnational (and thus publicly unaccountable) private interests carry out political and economic decision-making. Economic prosperity becomes narrowly defined as that condition by which corporations can function free of any government regulation of their bottom line while relying on government intervention in the form of tax breaks, corporate welfare, and related business assistance.

Under the Clinton Doctrine's ideological mandate, international exchange and public diplomacy have become useful tools to promote free trade, American competitiveness and U.S.-led "democracy building." This approach to cultural affairs is a marked contrast to what had at one time been described as the "soft" or non-adversarial dimension of international relations and foreign policy. Under the cold war umbrella, the interaction of individuals across cultures could often stand on its own merits, free of political and ideological competition. Now there is a hard sell behind the USIA.

The Clinton Doctrine is premised on the belief that the domestic strength of the United States is related to America's economic and military leadership abroad. As outlined in President Clinton's 1997 *National Security Strategy*, our national security core objectives are: (1) to enhance our security with effective diplomacy and with military forces that are ready to fight and to win; (2) to bolster America's economic prosperity; and (3) to promote democracy abroad. "To achieve these objectives, we will remain engaged abroad and work with partners, new and old, to promote peace and prosperity."[57]

Clinton's policy of engagement, as Noam Chomsky notes, is just an opportunity to continue corporate-state cooperation on economic and military strategies. It has very little to do with civil-based democratic society.

THE USIA'S FAILED MUTUAL UNDERSTANDING MISSION

While most Americans may tend to view the USIA's promotion of American market expansion as unproblematic, consider the legislation which established the U.S. Information Agency. Both the Smith-Mundt Act of

1948 and the Fulbright-Hays Act (otherwise known as the Mutual Educational and Cultural Exchange Act of 1961) were enacted to promote mutual understanding between the people of the United States and the people of other countries.

Mutual understanding carries with it a secondary mandate, which is part of the Agency's history but practically forgotten today. The USIA may be the government's official propaganda agency, but it has a second function: to teach Americans about other countries through its educational and cultural programs. In other words, exchange in principle is two-way: Americans have just as much to learn from other countries as they do to teach other countries.

President Jimmy Carter tried to resurrect the second mandate of the USIA, to teach Americans about the world, by changing the name of the agency to reflect a less nationalistic tone. It was renamed the United States International Communication Agency (ICA) and the signs proclaiming the motto that had served the USIA for twenty-five years, "Telling America's Story to the World," were removed from the agency's headquarters.

Carter declared the ICA mission one that would "undertake no activities which are covert, manipulative, or propagandistic. The agency can assume—as our founding fathers did—that a great and free society is its own best witness, and can put its faith in the power of ideas."[58] Anti-communist programming was curtailed, and the Agency's worldwide publication, "Problems of Communism," lost its circulation while other books that emphasized Third-world culture emerged.

In place of one-way ideology, Carter proposed a new educational mission for the new Agency: "To reduce the degree to which misperceptions and misunderstandings complicate relations between the United States and other nations. It is also in our interest—and in the interest of other nations—that Americans have the opportunity to understand the histories, cultures, and problems of others, so that we can come to understand their hopes, perceptions, and aspirations."[59] Carter's new vision for the ICA may have come from a Christian conviction that the United States was a nation needing a few lessons from others. In his Inaugural Address he stated, "We have learned that more is not necessarily better, that even our great nation has recognized limits." By the end of his presidency, he was blaming Americans for a hedonistic ethic that was defined more by what one owns than by what one does.

It would take Ronald Reagan's "Morning in America" message and a new USIA Director, close Reagan friend, and colorful former Hollywood press agent and producer Charles Wick, to reinvigorate the propagandistic mission of the USIA. Wick immediately reclaimed the one-way propaganda orientation of the Agency and revived its strong anti-Soviet message through "Project Truth" campaigns authorized by the National Security Council. The USIA's original name returned in 1982 and Wick called for volunteers from the academic community to help him detect Soviet "themes" of disinformation so that the USIA could help refute those themes. A new cold war of words was declared. Wick enlisted the help of *Commentary* magazine editor Norman Podhoretz and Edwin Feulner Jr., the president of the conservative Heritage Foundation, to spearhead a group of 17 volunteers from conservative backgrounds.[60] Under Wick, the Agency's budget mushroomed by 42% in its first fiscal year, stabilizing at around $1 billion by 1989 where it hovers today.[61]

In 1983 the USIA initiated "Project Democracy," an $85 million plan to "advocate the principles of democracy" at the same time the Reagan Administration was proposing a $100 million increase in arms aid to El Salvador. The project was met with widespread skepticism for including CIA Director William Casey in its planning meeting. Academics, once again, declared it too much of a hard sell. Nevertheless, Project Democracy graduated to become the National Endowment for Democracy. NED helps fledgling democracies through U.S. taxpayer funds funneled through the Republican and Democratic national parties, the U.S. Chamber of Commerce, and the AFL-CIO.

Ultimately Wick's tenure at the USIA became controversial as information emerged that the USIA's promotion of democracy was perhaps better served overseas than within its own walls. Wick had allegedly taped some phone conversations without the consent of the other party, and shortly thereafter, someone in the Agency had drawn up a blacklist of 84 liberals forbidden from taking part in USIA-sponsored speaker programs overseas.[62] When journalists started asking questions, agency management destroyed the blacklist.

After Wick's tenure, Henry Catto, the USIA Director under Bush, continued the "democracy-building" initiatives of the Reagan/Wick tenure. In a speech before the National Endowment for Democracy, Catto announced that the USIA would work with NED and a member of its family, the Center for International Private Enterprise (CIPE), to publish the quarterly *Economic Reform Today*. "Other government agencies are hard at work drafting the grand architecture of the New World Order; we're out there providing the nuts and bolts. What is private property? What is profit? How do I start a business? How do I learn English? How can my voice be heard in local affairs? These are the kinds of questions that ordinary people increasingly are asking around the world. And increasingly, USIA is providing the answers."[63]

The USIA's second mandate, to teach Americans about other countries, has been circumscribed by the 50-year-old Smith-Mundt prohibition that prevents the USIA from using propaganda on its own citizens. This explains why most Americans are unaware of the U.S. Information Agency, much less any of its programs. While anyone with a modem and access to the Internet can eventually locate the USIA website, Agency employees cannot disseminate USIA materials to Americans nor assist Americans in gaining access to the USIA Internet addresses. Why does this clearly outmoded ban continue in 1998? Many members of Congress, including Senator Jesse Helms, worry about propaganda programs, designed for overseas audiences, being used for domestic purposes. It is also thought that the most powerful lobby in Washington, the National Association of Broadcasters, along with its supporters in Congress, does not want any competition from a government-owned but quasi-independent Voice of America broadcast like the BBC in Britain.

The Smith-Mundt ban challenges the First Amendment rights of U.S. citizens who underwrite the billion-dollar propaganda programs of the USIA. Such a ban makes it nearly impossible for the American public to weigh in its opposition to, or continued support of, taxpayer-funded USIA programs. Granted, the original intent of the ban's passage after World War II was to prevent the U.S. government from propagandizing its own people, a noble purpose. But in a global information age where geographical boundaries are fast becoming meaningless through the World Wide Web, this outmoded ban should be lifted to allow global access to USIA archival materials. Some public interest groups, notably Essential Information and the Center for Study of Responsive Law, are fighting the Smith-Mundt ban in the courts.

In *Essential Information, et al., v. United States Information Agency,* plaintiffs argue for American public access to USIA archival material and to its Internet addresses. (Currently the USIA claims that its Internet addresses are designed only for an overseas audience.) These include the Voice of America; WORLDNET, the USIA's satellite television network; the USIA Wireless File, a daily text-based press service, produced in five languages and linked by computerized communication systems to all overseas USIS posts; and numerous USIA publications, in both printed and electronic form, which deal with market democracies, trade, security, and other transnational issues.

The U.S. Congress has authorized the USIA to use broadcast technologies that have a spillover effect on an American audience. Thus, Radio and TV Martí, which broadcast to Cuba, can be received in parts of southern Florida. Voice of America broadcasts can be received on shortwave radio in the United States and WORLDNET television broadcasts can be received by anyone in the U.S. with a satellite dish. But the Smith-Mundt ban requires that the USIA not actively encourage domestic use of its materials, which according to the plaintiffs in the lawsuit against the USIA, provides preferential access to foreigners and those living outside the United States.

It creates irrational situations whereby a U.S. citizen residing along the Canadian border could theoretically drive to Canada, pick up USIS materials from the U.S. embassy, and return to the U.S. with the materials, all within the law. That same U.S. citizen cannot simply call up USIA headquarters in Washington, DC, and request the same materials because those materials are designed for those living outside the United States.

THE USIA'S BUSINESS-FRIENDLY MISSION

Despite this domestic ban on dissemination of propaganda to a U.S. audience, the USIA has actively courted the U.S. business community under the Clinton administration's trade-first approach to foreign policy. During my tenure at the agency, the USIA sponsored two high-profile conferences designed to build commercial ties between the United States and commercial partners overseas.

The USIA organized its first conference, "Partnership for Progress: U.S.-NIS Conference on Democracy and the Market Economy," in October 1993 in St. Louis to link U.S. business executives with government officials and entrepreneurs of the former Soviet Union. The mood at the gathering was ebullient. Lawrence Summers, undersecretary for international affairs at the U.S. Treasury Department, told the gathering that Russia's privatization program "is a huge success. The days are gone when Russians stood three hours a day in line in the hope of purchasing some basic necessity." Summers warned against a go-slow approach to Russian reforms. This is "bad politics, bad economics, and a bad interpretation of the experience of the countries in transition." He urged Russia to speed up its reforms by moving quickly to create a legal framework for property rights and to respect contracts. "These are critical steps needed not only for Russian business but also for encouraging foreign investment."[64]

In June 1994, the USIA sponsored "Investing in People: The U.S.–South Africa Conference on Democracy and Economic Development," where 400 business leaders, Commerce Department officials, and members of Congress met their South African counterparts for two days of deal-making in Atlanta. Said Vice President Gore at the meeting: "The key to the future of South Africa and our relationship will be the private sector. That's where the long-term jobs will be created. That's what will create the infrastructure. That's what will create the income."[65] *Washington Post* staff writer Kenneth J. Cooper described the business conference as "unusual because the host was the federal government and it had diplomatic as well as financial objectives in mind." Just weeks after this June 3-4 meeting, the USIA coordinated a White House Conference on Africa at the behest of the National Security Council.

Why all this focus on Africa? A USIS Washington File article, "Africa: One of the 'Last Frontiers' for U.S. Business," said it all: "The continent of Africa now stands as one of the last international frontiers offering opportunities and 'untapped markets' for American businesses and foreign investors willing to take up the challenge."[66]

But most revealing were statements by Jeffrey Donald, special assistant to the coordinator for business affairs at the U.S. State Department. "For a while during the cold war period, our support for American commercial interests diminished at the State Department. We focused heavily on the political and ideological competition with the former Soviet Union, often to the detriment of American business. With the end of the cold war, however, there has been a dramatic shift in the department's emphasis on support for American business." Donald explained that attention to business has continued with the creation of the America Desk Initiative under former Secretary of State Warren Christopher "which called upon State Department officers to integrate vital concerns of American business into our foreign policy process."

This business slant in foreign policy became evident at USIA where it became increasingly necessary for us to justify educational and cultural exchanges by linking their success to American business and economic development goals. A memorandum was once circulated to all USIA employees to help us explain to Congress and the press how cultural exchange programs supported U.S. foreign economic development interests.

By emphasizing U.S. business and commercial values, the USIA's mission comes across as narrow and exploitative to many people around the world whose aspirations are directly challenging U.S.-led economic liberalization programs. As Jeff Faux explained in *The Nation*, "The most popular U.S. export is Hollywood movies. The second most popular export is also a bit of fantasy: the idea that the U.S. economy is a model for how other market economies—developed and less developed—can successfully adapt to the global marketplace."[67]

THE USIA AND NAFTA: BUILDING A FOUNDATION FOR SUCCESS?

While the USIA continues to coordinate the U.S. government's educational and cultural exchanges, it is clear that mutual understanding is being undermined by the expansion of market interests. Nowhere is this better illustrated than with the USIA's role in promoting the North American Free Trade Agreement (NAFTA) in the fall of 1993 and its continued public relations campaign for American competitiveness and global integration through the World Trade Organization (WTO).

During the full-court press for NAFTA, the U.S. propaganda machine was in full tilt. An internal USIA report, "USIA and NAFTA: Building a Foundation for Success," glowed that public diplomacy had been "central" to the implementation process of NAFTA. "We worked to show the most influential segments of Mexican society that U.S. interests in Mexico ran much deeper than mere profit margins. By nurturing American interest in and respect for Mexican intellectual and cultural values and accomplishments, we could build a social base for economic and political cooperation while disarming Mexico's greatest potential opposition to NAFTA."[68] The building of that social base was made easier by the fact that then-President Salinas, six of his senior cabinet colleagues, and his top three NAFTA negotiators had received training and education in the United States, many under the USIA–sponsored Fulbright program.[69]

The USIA proposed, and the Mexican government accepted, the establishment of a bilateral Fulbright Commission in Mexico in 1990, which extended U.S. financial interests in the area. Over the next three years, private representatives from both countries joined the Commission, which would facilitate programs such as the Fullbright/Coca-Cola Environmental Scholars Program.[70] By the fall of 1993, the USIA-sponsored NAFTA efforts were in full swing. In the weeks leading up to the NAFTA vote in the U.S. Congress, USIS-Mexico sponsored six congressional delegations and visits by governors and university presidents, briefed visiting U.S. journalists, and shared USIA polling data with American CEOs "who thought, erroneously, that Mexico is an anti-American country."[71] The USIA also laid claim to having transformed the once Marxist-leaning economics department at the National University in an effort to "alter the strategic perspective on bilateral relations and open channels for constructive and stabilizing cooperation."[72]

In contrast to Mexico, selling NAFTA to the Canadians is characterized as an uphill struggle in the USIA NAFTA document. Canadian public opinion was generally anti-NAFTA. The USIA describes Canada's relationship with the U.S. as "stubbornly ambivalent," particularly regarding American cultural imperialism.[73] "Canadian opinion was quick to identify free trade with the erosion of national institutions and values, including corporations absorbed by American-dominated multinationals as well as by cultural, media, and entertainment industries dominated by U.S. products and control."[74]

The response by the USIA was to have USIS-Canada organize briefings for American and Canadian journalists to present "the full story" on free trade, and sponsor bilateral initiatives like the 1993 conference on "Trade and the Environment" at Carleton University in Ottawa and the 1993-94 Worldnet interactive television series on "The Information Superhighway in North America." The USIA report declares NAFTA victory in Canada in classic propagandistic rhetoric: "By October 1993 the significance of NAFTA in the approaching Canadian elections demanded that the USIA's programming on that topic essentially stop. The program continued to explain

NAFTA-related developments in the U.S., but direct, pro-free trade programming stopped. While public support for free trade continued to be soft, there was no expectation that Canada would turn its back on NAFTA. The die was set: Canadians understood that the free trade train had left the station and they did not want to be left behind. The USIA's persistent efforts to describe North America's post-cold war future as one best faced by maximizing the benefits of economic interdependence through free trade were surely a positive factor in Canadian acquiescence to, if not great enthusiasm for, NAFTA."[75]

The USIA's efforts notwithstanding, Canadian criticism of NAFTA has persisted. The "Red Book" of Liberal party objectives stated in 1993 that "culture is the very essence of national identity, the bedrock of national sovereignty and national pride—Canada needs more than ever to commit itself to cultural development. Instead the Conservative regime has deliberately undermined our national cultural institutions."[76] The Liberal government of Prime Minister Jean Chretien won on that issue of cultural sovereignty and yet accepted a free trade agreement that did not exempt culture.

In an open letter to Prime Minister Jean Chretien, former senior trade negotiator Mel Clark accused the Canadian government of perpetuating the myth that Canada's cultural institutions are protected by the terms of NAFTA. On the contrary, Clark argues, the purpose of NAFTA was to serve U.S. interests and speed up the Americanization of Canadian culture.[77] Further, the Canadian Centre for Policy Alternatives released data in 1997 indicating that most of the large Canadian corporations that promised to create more and better jobs after the Canada–U.S. Free Trade Agreement (FTA) was signed in 1988, significantly reduced their work forces. Thirty-three of the largest corporations cut 216,000 jobs or about 35% of their original work force between 1988 and 1996. During that period, these same 33 companies increased their combined annual revenues by more than $40 billion, a rise of more than 34%. The Canadian public in 1988, like the American public in 1993, was assured in a massive media blitz financed by large corporate backers that free trade would translate into the hiring of many more workers at higher wages.

THE USIA AND THE USA*NAFTA CONNECTION

A missing link in the USIA report about NAFTA promotion is the central role played by one intimately tied to the top tier of the Agency. In June 1993, President Clinton appointed American University President Joseph Duffey to become Director of the U.S. Information Agency. Duffey emerged on the scene at a time in which the entire culture of the federal foreign affairs bureaucracy was changing from one steeped in a political-military tradition to one driven by economic and commercial engagement.[78] Duffey's appointment to head the USIA is not nearly as significant as his wife's influential lobbying position, particularly on the issue of NAFTA passage in Congress.

Duffey's wife, Anne Wexler, is head of the Wexler Group, a top Washington lobbying firm and registered foreign agent. The January 1998 issue of *Washingtonian* magazine names Wexler the top female lobbyist in Washington, D.C. "She is easily the most influential female lobbyist in a world still dominated by men. An avid golfer, Wexler can often be seen on the links at the Army-

Navy Club playing with her husband, Joseph Duffey, head of the United States Information Agency."[79]

According to a 1996 report by the Center for Public Integrity, Wexler has been an adviser to President Clinton ever since he first campaigned as a president who would end "influence peddling" and "business as usual" in Washington.[80] Wexler helped prepare the campaign's health-care briefing books while representing health-care industry interests. Her clients include ARCO, AT&T, the Cellular Telecommunications Industry Association, Eastman Kodak, the Heinz Family Foundation, Johnson & Johnson, Ohio Edison, Pitney Bowes, Inc., and Sega of America.

The Wexler Group lobby represented the pro-NAFTA business coalition of Fortune 500 companies known as USA*NAFTA. The 1995 Project Censored Yearbook, *Censored: The News That Didn't Make the News and Why*, identified the broken promises of USA*NAFTA as one of the top ten censored stories of the year. "Two years after NAFTA's narrow passage, the 200,000 new jobs promised by the trade brokers are nowhere to be found, pollution has increased in Mexico, and workers across the border are spraying more toxic pesticides on fruits, vegetables, and people than ever. Nevertheless, USA*NAFTA, a coalition led by Fortune 500 companies that helped push through NAFTA, has suffered neither negative publicity nor political disfavor."[81] Drawing on two analyses by progressive publications, "NAFTA's Broken Promises" describes how the hard-sell promises of Wexler's USA*NAFTA coalition for increased wages, reductions in illegal immigration, improvements in the Mexican environment, and high-paying U.S. jobs had become underreported broken promises. Just two years later, Mexican emigration to the U.S. increased by 30 percent, the peso devaluation crisis of December 1994 cut the value of Mexican wages by as much as 40 percent (making Mexican consumers much less able to buy U.S. imports), and the U.S. trade surplus with Mexico turned into a trade deficit of over $6 billion.[82] By May 1995, NAFTA's promises were a net job destroyer for U.S. workers. Further, USA*NAFTA businesses were shown to be "corporate con artists" for referring to their efforts as a grassroots organization. In fact, the pro-NAFTA business coalition represented the boardrooms of the largest American multinational interests and not the living rooms of the average American homes.[83]

On July 11, 1997, the Clinton Administration released a report on NAFTA's first three years and humbly stated that what USA*NAFTA had promised in hundreds of thousands of new American jobs, higher wages, and a cleaner environment was in reality a "modest positive effect." Positive for multinational corporations. The losers were workers and environmental health and safety.

As David Bonior reported in the *New York Times*, Mexican wages along the border declined from $1 to 70 cents an hour according to IMF figures.[84] A 1996 Cornell University study commissioned by the U.S. Labor Department showed that 62 percent of U.S. companies surveyed admitted to using the threat of moving to Mexico to keep wages low at home. Less than one percent of the 3.3 million Mexican trucks entering the U.S. southern border are inspected, according to a May 1997 General Accounting Office study. This bodes well for the cocaine trafficking across the U.S.-Mexico border but threatens the U.S. population with uninspected produce carrying pesticides, disease, and parasites. However, tightening inspections of imported produce is considered an unfair trade restriction under NAFTA. And the winners? Those same corporations which formed a buddy system under USA*NAFTA, contracted with the Wexler Group, and lobbied hard for NAFTA passage in 1993. A significant 42 percent of these corporations moved jobs overseas after NAFTA, according to Labor Department trade adjustment assistance data, and their profits jumped by 296 percent, this according to financial data published in *Forbes* magazine. Not a bad return on their initial investment.

The activities of Wexler's USA*NAFTA and Duffey's USIA on behalf of NAFTA exemplify a troubling trend in so-called public-private partnerships in general and the USIA's mission in particular. "Public-private partnership" has become a catchy Clinton Administration slogan. It sounds good and suggests a new streamlined government that avoids duplication and increases efficiency. In reality, as the USA*NAFTA model shows, public-private partnership is a means by which corporations protect and expand their own interests through propaganda campaigns that circumvent democratic dialogue and control.

USIA's purpose is informational and cultural. As a propaganda machine its purpose includes advocacy on behalf of U.S. government and client (i.e. business) interests. On the other hand, as an educational and cultural affairs agency, its purpose is also "to increase mutual understanding" and to educate Americans about how the rest of the world lives. The USIA's advocacy on behalf of NAFTA served only an informational and propagandistic purpose. It did nothing to advance the more noble goals of mutual understanding and education.

When the Clinton Administration was pressing for fast-track trade authority in 1997, the Wexler Group got the contract again. Working with the same pro-NAFTA corporate firms in a new coalition, America Leads on Trade (ALOT), they claimed that fast-track trade authority would, like NAFTA, mean more jobs for America's workers. The coalition of 450 corporations and 120 trade associations aired TV commercials in Congressional swing districts, despite public opinion polls showing 60 percent opposition to fast-track approval.

A study published jointly by the Institute for Policy Studies and United for a Fair Economy revealed that a significant number of ALOT members did not live up to their rhetoric. The report, "Who Benefits from Fast Track?: A Study of Corporate Free Trade Lobby," used Department of Labor statistics to show that 40 ALOT members had cut jobs at 89 plants, laying off nearly 13,000 workers who qualified for a NAFTA retraining program. The CEOs at the top ALOT firms earned significantly more than the already high average of leading U.S. executives, and profits of these 40 job-slashing firms soared under NAFTA, rising by 335 percent between 1992 and 1996 compared to a 68 percent rise for Fortune 500 companies as a whole. The same blue chip companies that promised positive employment benefits from NAFTA—Allied-Signal, General Electric, General Motors, Johnson & Johnson, Proctor and Gamble, Sara Lee, Whirlpool, Siemens, and Xerox—laid off workers under NAFTA. General Electric was the top ALOT downsizer, with 2,318 workers certified for NAFTA retraining, despite leading the claim in 1993 that NAFTA would boost trade that "could support 10,000 jobs for GE and its suppliers." In 1996, GE could provide no evidence of any job creation; nevertheless, Jack Welch had take-home pay in 1996 of $27 million in salary and bonuses.

ALOT's alter ego, USA ENGAGE, is a corporate coalition that wants to engage every country in the world, no matter how much the U.S. public might disapprove of a particular country's human rights records. The cast of characters includes American Express, ARCO, AT&T, Bank America, Boeing, Caterpillar, Chase Manhattan, and Chrysler, the same names which appear on the lists of top money donors to the Republican and Democratic party coffers. What Jim Hightower calls "a one-world pep group," USA ENGAGE consists of 632 corporate entities that support making it illegal for local city councils or state legislatures to pass any law that would impede American business engagements with some of the top human rights abusers in the world. Several U.S. states, plus about 30 counties and cities, have adopted their own purchasing rules that prohibit doing business with corporations that engage with democracy-challenged countries like China or Burma. USA ENGAGE would like to outlaw existing local and state expression of the people's will and prevent further legislation but a citizen coalition against these corporate front groups seems to be gaining momentum.

The postponement of fast-track trade legislation in Congress was a sign that progressives, labor unions, environmentalists, consumer and church groups that had fought hard to defeat NAFTA, worked effectively this time with workers frustrated by the unrealized promises of the corporate trade agenda. *The Nation* editorialized that "contrary to the hysterical warnings of fast-track proponents, the vote does not represent the triumph of a dying isolationism but of a new internationalism. It is not the end of U.S. leadership but a call for leading in a different direction. It will not undermine the forces of freedom across the world, as Secretary of State Madeleine Albright ranted, but is a call to put America's weight on the side of worker, consumer, and environmental movements globally. It won't threaten prosperity, imperil the market or trigger trade wars, as the corporate lobby predicted; it may in fact be a necessary first step toward saving global capital from its own excesses."[85] The *Toronto Star* reported, "If 'globaphobia' leads the United States to address the legitimate concerns of ordinary workers and their families, this is a good thing."[86]

WHITHER THE USIA UNDER CLINTON?

In 1992, candidate Clinton ran a campaign with a theme of "putting people first" that included the popular and much memorialized motto, "It's the economy, stupid." Clinton challenged the cold war legacy of Reagan and Bush and spoke of an opportunity to shift focus from national security, containment, and foreign affairs to domestic programs like health care and education that would benefit all Americans.

Less than one year later, President Clinton was running a new campaign, putting markets first, and the *Wall Street Journal* and *New York Times* editorial pages were singing the praises of this pro-business New Democrat. As chief international affairs correspondent for the *New York Times*, Thomas Friedman explained: "America's victory in the cold war was a victory for a set of political and economic principles: democracy and the free market. The free market is the wave of the future—a future for which America is both the gatekeeper and model."[87]

The first success of this new policy was the passage of the North American Free Trade Agreement (NAFTA) and the new World Trade Organization, which included a Bill of Rights of economic protections for global corporations. The people, who had so much rhetorical significance to candidate Clinton, were replaced by a trade *über Alles* approach to foreign policy, with the promise that if U.S. corporate interests were emphasized, the people's prosperity would follow.

By April 1997 the Clinton Administration announced the end of the cold war era in foreign affairs to correspond with another era's end, big government. In order to streamline the Executive Branch's ability to meet the growing foreign policy challenges of the 21st century, Clinton announced that matters of international arms control, sustainable development, and public diplomacy would be placed within a reinvented State Department.

The USIA is scheduled to be incorporated into the State Department by October 1999.[88] The USIA's current information programs will be integrated with public affairs in the State Department, a new State Department bureau created to handle cultural and exchange issues, and a new assistant secretary of public diplomacy added to ease the transition. This move, however, suggests business-as-usual for the Clinton Administration and the USIA. As outlined by Nancy Soderberg, foreign policy adviser to the National Security Council, economic prosperity remains one of the main priorities of Clinton's second term. In an address to the National Democratic Club in December 1996, Soderberg predicted continued efforts by the Administration to develop "a new global trading system with America at its hub."[89]

In a statement released prior to his May 1997 Business Development Mission to Latin America, Commerce Secretary Daley echoed that sentiment. "The United States government will stand shoulder-to-shoulder with its business community in a vigorous public-private partnership. Our resources and efforts will help companies secure export opportunities that represent the largest potential source of high-paying jobs in the next century. The message to the U.S. business community is also clear: The Clinton Administration will advocate forcefully on their behalf."[90] His words reflect the commercial diplomacy efforts that late Commerce Secretary Ron Brown turned into a controversial but high art form. In a speech at Howard University, Brown said that commercial engagement is a vehicle that advances "not only economic but strategic and social objectives. Building commerce between nations encourages the exchange of products and capital, of course. But it also encourages the exchange of ideas and ideals."[91]

The USIA's future strategy emphasizes public-private partnership and reinventing itself through "collecting, evaluating and using performance data to improve our program results."[92] Once again, public-private partnership is government doublespeak for private domination and public acquiescence in budget-cutting times. Under this context, foreign trade and economic policy are fully partnered with U.S. cultural and information policy. As pressure increases for the USIA to measure its performance, a "good" USIA program is one led by bottom line corporate considerations: Does it expand American markets? Does it promote American competitiveness? Does it link American business to overseas counterparts? Mutual understanding becomes a straw man concept by which the U.S. government, coached by business, informs and influences while other countries listen and understand.

Current public diplomacy and foreign policy making reduces the role of American citizens to mere spectators. The USIA's model of democracy and the free market is promoted as the superpower version of economic globalization, packaged and ready for shipping to clients throughout the world. In this version, foreign capital flows freely while the movement of people, particularly the world's poor, is strictly monitored and controlled.[93] Such a commercial package speaks first and foremost for government "partners," the Fortune 500 corporations, which are the primary beneficiaries as well as the bankrollers of the American political process. This is a packaged story of America that is incomplete and undemocratic. Where do workers and communities fit into the story? How do private citizens play a part in building dialogue across cultures?

There is strong evidence that the USIA is an ineffective, obsolete agency that should be dismantled. The USIA has no legitimate post–cold war function and primarily serves the interests of U.S. trade and economic sectors by touting to foreign elite audiences the superiority of U.S. commercial values and the soundness of U.S. economic policies. Likewise, by overplaying foreign economic concerns, the USIA neglects its second mandate, citing Smith-Mundt restraints that prohibit the American public from having access to USIA materials. The USIA's operation, like a mini-Commerce Department, makes for duplication of government services in a post-big-government era of downsizing and budget cuts. Finally, private huckster-ism for U.S. business interests under the rhetoric of "public" diplomacy makes a mockery of agency mandates for mutual understanding between the people of the U.S. and the people of other countries.

Progressive arguments in favor of abolishing the USIA include some unusual company. The Cato Institute, a conservative think tank, supports the elimination of the USIA but for other reasons: "Since the end of the cold war, there is less and less appropriate government action to take. The United States no longer needs to combat communism by, for example, supporting trade unionism, cranking out propaganda, or giving out scholarships to foreign students. In contrast, as a growing number of economies open up to trade and investment, there is more and more commercial and financial (i.e. nongovernmental) action to take. Given the enormous impact of Hollywood, Motown, Levi's, hundreds of thousands of travelers, and the news media, it is hard to believe that U.S. government information and cultural programs could make anything but the most marginal impressions on the minds of foreigners. Moreover, it makes little sense to send American culture abroad for free when foreign populations are clearly willing to pay for it. There is no longer a need to 'win their hearts and minds.'"[94]

I favor a political democracy and foreign policy driven by informed citizen activists. The USIA's function, like the mini–Commerce Department it has become, is to sell one version of America, essentially corporate, to the influential dominant markets of the world. But America's legacy has never been and will never be just for the selling. Countless American citizens, working with their counterparts abroad, are using their united vision to promote a global civic society which promotes a one-world community—not a one-world market—where diverse cultures can work together in efforts to combat poverty, oppression, pollution, and collective violence.

In contrast to the USIA's boardroom-style globalization model, many of these citizen activists favor more freedom of movement for people and greater regulation of capital. A classical economic philosophy and its almost messianic devotion to unlimited growth do not drive this global grassroots system. Instead, it takes into account people's values, their cultural and natural environments, and local economies where traditional non-market values like reciprocity, mutual aid, and self-reliance build community bonds.

ROADBLOCKS ON THE PATH TO A NEW FOREIGN POLICY

One of the major roadblocks on the path to citizen-based diplomacy is that big business and big money rule the American system of democracy. We don't need an independent counsel or special prosecutor to point this out to us. Instead of one person, one vote, we have a system of one dollar, one vote. The two dominant parties, Republican and Democrat, are what Ralph Nader likes to call a "duopoly." This two-party monopoly is represented by the same large corporations that form business coalitions like USA*NAFTA, USA*ENGAGE, or ALOT. Neither party has the moral courage to take on the private system of financing our politics because each is beholden to corporate money and special interests in a never-ending cycle of cash and influence.

Many myths perpetuate that confuse the American people about who is really running campaigns. During the 1996 campaign, conservatives charged that the Clinton Administration was controlled by organized labor, failing to mention that the lion's share of money for both Republicans and Democrats is business.

A November 1997 report by the Center for Responsive Politics indicated that in 1996 "business outspent labor by a factor of 11 to one and ideological groups by 19 to one," and "nearly two-thirds of the business money went to Republicans," which has fed a growing dependence among Democrats on organized labor.[95] Despite the dominance of business interests in campaign finance, another pro-business coalition, run out of the Chamber of Commerce of the United States, is gearing up for the 1998 elections to fight the AFL-CIO. Calling itself, "The Coalition: Americans Working for Real Change," it raised $5 million in the 1996 election to combat organized labor's advertising campaign. Now the Coalition wants to permanently fight any attempts to establish a labor-oriented Congress. Congress remains "pro-business but by the narrowest of margins.... A handful of new anti-business members or weaknesses among pro-business members could stop progress toward a smaller federal government, lower and simpler taxes, tort reform, free trade, and workplace regulatory reform dead in its tracks."[96] The Coalition's client list includes the National Restaurant Association, the National Association of Manufacturers, and the National Federation of Independent Businesses, many of whose individual members give generous soft money contributions to mostly the Republican party and who actively oppose any attempts to pass campaign finance reform legislation which would limit their access to government.

Another problem is that the people, traditionally represented by their government, find themselves facing a new power—global corporations—which hold no allegiance to any one individual, community, or place. A revealing study by the Institute for Policy Studies, using World Bank and U.N. data from 1995, indicated that 51 of the 100 largest economies in the world were corporations. Only 49 were countries. They included Mitsubishi (22nd), General Motors (26), Ford Motor (31), Exxon (39), Wal-Mart (42) and AT&T (48). These top 200 corporations' combined sales surpassed the combined economies of 182 countries. Wal-Mart alone had sales in 1995 that were greater than the GNP of 161 countries.[97]

What this means is that we are growing up in a society today where big government is being downsized while the power of global corporations is concentrating and coalescing across national boundaries (thus their name "transnational corporations" or TNCs). Despite this trend, our media (particularly conservative talk radio) continue to emphasize stories that point to the U.S. government as the most dominant and controlling institution in society. Even President Clinton acknowledged in his 1996 State of the Union address to great bipartisan applause that "the era of big government is over." But these same media, our top elected official, and our two dominant political parties rarely criticize the growing power of large corporations because they are bankrolled by them.[98]

Democracies thrive only when power is deconcentrated from the hands of a few to many. Thomas Jefferson warned that "banking institutions and moneyed incorporations," if given free reign to dominate the people, could destroy democracy. The 20th-century social philosopher John Dewey could have been talking about the late 20th century when he said: "Power today resides in control of the means of production, exchange, publicity, transportation and communication. Whoever owns them rules the life of a country." Politics becomes then "the shadow cast on society by big business," so long as the country is ruled by "business for private profit through private control of banking, land, industry, reinforced by command of the press, press agents, and other means of publicity and propaganda."[99]

Against a backdrop of growing corporate power it is understandable that many Americans feel powerless to change political institutions. They see their own government merging the public with the private sector in service of the private sector's interests. We grow up corporate-minded, leading the sponsored life, but are ignorant about many of our civic rights.

One of these central rights Americans have is to be informed and engaged by *our* media. It is well known and readily understood that our major broadcast media are advertising-supported and profit-driven. What is little known and less understood is that the American people own the airwaves. Since 1934 our federal government has freely given radio and television broadcasters the right to use the public airwaves for private gain as long as they promote the public's interest. And what is the public interest? Broadly defined, that media inform and engage the public in order to increase citizen participation in the democratic process. An uninformed citizenry cannot make sound decisions about power relations and resource allocation, which are so central to political decision-making. It is then critically important that our major media inform the citizenry and promote political participation in the democratic process. The problem lies with ownership and concentration.

In 1983, when Ben Bagdikian first published *The Media Monopoly*, his now classic critique of the America media environment, he reported that 50 corporations controlled most of the American media in newspapers, television and radio, book publishing and movie studios. His criticism of the harmful effects of corporate-owned and advertising-driven news earned him a reputation as an "alarmist." His 1992 edition reported that 50 had shrunk to 20. Bagdikian's 5th edition was published on April 1, 1997, but there's no April Fools joke here: What were 50 corporations fourteen years ago is down to 10 media conglomerates that dominate the U.S. system.[100] What Bagdikian calls a "horror" is unconscionable to anyone concerned with the democratic process.

A 1997 Common Cause study, "Channeling Influence: The Broadcast Lobby and the $70-billion Free Ride," provides a picture of the power these major media wield in the halls of Congress. Each programmer now holds a license to use a portion of the public airwaves to broadcast radio and television. Emerging digital technology will increase the economic value of that spectrum system and allow broadcasters access to multi-use programming. Traditional television sets will be replaced with digital "genies" which offer a higher quality picture and sound along with computer data, paging and cellular service. Broadcasters have lobbied hard to use the new digital spectrum for free. The Federal Communications Commission, the U.S. government arm which oversees the broadcast industry, estimates that the new digital TV licenses, if auctioned off to broadcasters, would generate at least $70 billion for the federal treasury. Unfortunately the FCC is not likely to put undue pressure on broadcasters to pay. FCC officials tend to be industry supporters instead of public defenders of the airwaves.

On January 8, 1918, President Woodrow Wilson gave

his Fourteen Points Speech for world peace which outlined "a general association of nations," the precursor to the United Nations. In this age of globalization of finance capital, the acquiescence of governments to corporate power and control, and the continued domination of transnational structures like the IMF, World Bank, GATT, and NAFTA, it is time, some 80 years later, to form a united, autonomous association of citizen movements which can resist the marketization of human lives and their environment. The following, my more modest 7-Point Plan for a citizen-based diplomacy, is influenced by the efforts of citizen groups working with progressive politicians to launch a "Fairness Agenda for America" in response to the corporate-defined Republican "Contract with America."[101]

7-POINT PLAN FOR A CITIZEN-BASED DIPLOMACY

1. RESTORE THE BODY POLITIC. A citizen-based diplomacy places civic-mindedness and civic activism at the center of our body politic by emphasizing human rights, human security, and environmental and cultural preservation. The current body politic emphasizes economic theories, glorifies the free market, and reduces the role of citizens to occasional endorsers of winner-take-all options. A new body politic takes into account the interests and concerns of citizens affected by global policymaking. Public opinion polls consistently show support for demilitarization and a shift in foreign policy from arms sales and exports to economic and social justice. A new body politic demands that its government resist efforts by military contractors and lobbyists to look for new markets for their wares, and pressures government to convert a military-dependent economy that benefits a few large conglomerates to a self-sustaining energy-efficient economy that benefits all.

2. FIGHT "TRADE ÜBER ALLES" FOREIGN POLICY. Foreign policy is no longer the exclusive domain of economic and military elites. Just ask Jody Williams, U.S. coordinator of the International Campaign to Ban Landmines, a coalition of over 1,000 organizations in 60 countries which worked with receptive governments to redefine international norm and international law. Williams attributes the campaign's success to working outside the bounds of major institutions like the United Nations where the anti-landmine campaign had stalled and to building networks with citizen groups and smaller pro-ban countries. The Nobel Committee readily admitted that its decision to award the 1997 Nobel Peace Prize to Jody Williams and the ICBL was designed to pressure superpowers like the United States, Russia, and China to sign an international treaty banning the use of anti-personnel landmines.[102] That plan seemed to partially work. President Boris Yeltsin immediately announced that Russia would become a signatory to the international treaty. When President Clinton did not call to congratulate the American Nobel laureate, Williams understood why: "The message we've been sending this administration for the past few years is that they are on the wrong side of humanity. He knows what our message is. I would say the same thing to him on the telephone as I've said to him on TV."[103] Jody Williams never got a call from President Clinton, but the parents of septuplets in Iowa did.

Mass-based local movements, citizen deliberation

and debate put pressure on government and corporate elites to open the political process. That pressure can reshape foreign policy to cut current cold-war levels of military spending, convert military research and development initiatives to domestic social needs, stop arms-bazaar NATO expansion, shift from a unilateral military presence abroad to a multilateral response, and place human rights instead of expanding markets at the forefront of foreign policy.

3. REDEFINE FOREIGN ASSISTANCE. Despite the end of the cold war, foreign assistance continues to mean assisting countries in death and destruction in the form of weapons and ammunition. The United States is the world's remaining superpower, not only in economic and military strength, but also in arms trafficking. As long as foreign assistance remains defined by arms transfers, less developed countries that are in transition to democracy will remain vulnerable to military forces working with repressive governments that systematically violate human rights. Real foreign assistance would provide technology and resources to help grassroots organizations document human rights abuses on video and the Internet, report abuses in a timely fashion to news services, facilitate internal and international communication, and link their efforts to worldwide social movements.

4. EMPHASIZE PEOPLE AND PROGRESS, NOT MARKETS AND GROWTH. A citizen-based diplomacy challenges the secular economic god, "growth," its outmoded measure, GNP, and the myth of "free trade," which continue to dominate global economic policy despite irrefutable evidence that global human activity is destroying natural resources and creating inequalities both here and abroad. Redefining progress from growth to quality of life reveals that two-thirds of the world's people are still marginalized in the new global economy and the gap is widening between rich and poor in developed and less developed countries. Citizens must hold governments and corporations accountable for the inequities of the marketplace instead of hearing only of its virtues.

5. REDIGNIFY WORK AND LABOR. Economic globalization tends to define work and labor in employer terms: "flexible labor markets" where workers accept unconscionably low wages and dismal working conditions, or how work affects only the bottom line. A citizen-based diplomacy places work and labor at the center of the global economy debate, addresses economic anxiety in families and the workplace, and puts pressure on governments and their corporate patrons to promote an adequate living wage, safe working conditions, and a progressive tax structure based on individual or institutional ability to pay.

Take the example of the global citizen campaign against the Nike corporation. This highly profitable multinational corporation walked out on the American shoe industry. Nike does not have a single shoe factory within the United States, abandoning higher-wage American workers and their families for low-wage undemocratic countries like China, Indonesia, and Vietnam. Despite its feel-good, "Just Do It" corporate motto and well-publicized support for women in sports, Nike exploits women and children in labor camp conditions where pregnant women are routinely fired and women lose fingers in rushed assembly lines. So far Nike has been able to protect its good corporate citizen image by spending over $978 million in worldwide advertising in 1996 and flaunting its multimillion dollar endorsement contracts with popular sports figures like Michael Jordan and Tiger Woods. But efforts by progressive members of Congress to engage Nike C.E.O. Phil Knight in improving his labor practices overseas and expand his manufacturing to U.S. communitites may apply some extra public pressure for Nike and like-minded corporate citizens to "just do the right thing."

6. BROADEN DEFINITION OF DEMOCRACY THROUGH "CLEAN" ELECTIONS. A civic-based democracy supports reform movements to reduce the amount of private money in politics in the short-term and public financing of elections in the long-term to eliminate the need for elected public servants to be professional fund-raisers. Citizens are concerned that candidates spend most of their time chasing after big money and that well-qualified but under-funded candidates don't have a real chance of being elected. A clean money campaign reform approach is the most sweeping option available for citizens to reclaim their democracy from the reigns of private industry. It would, among other things, provide voluntary public financing for qualified candidates, ban the use of soft money (unregulated large money donations), provide free and discounted TV time for candidates who agree to spending limits (even President Clinton called for that in his 1998 State of the Union address), shorten the campaign season, and require full electronic disclosure. Such a system has already passed by ballot initiative in Maine and in the Vermont state legislature and similar measures are underway in dozens of U.S. states. The public financing option places citizens at the center of democratic debate and would likely lead to real democracy measures like civilian monitoring of military and intelligence budgets, an independent judiciary, and broader avenues for citizen redress and involvement in the political and economic decision making process.

7. SUPPORT MEDIA REFORM. The national commercial television networks have been less than vigilant in exposing how corporate money is corrupting American politics. The print media have done a better job in tracking fat cat contributions to both dominant parties, but the "Big Five" broadcasters (ABC, CBS, NBC, Fox and CNN) have not been beating their drums in support of campaign fincance reform. Why? Because they have a direct conflict of interest in the story. The national networks profit handsomely from the corrupt political process that drives campaigns. Most of the big money given to candidates running for national office ends up being spent on television ads and media consultants. In the 1996 elections, the top 75 media markets collected $400 million to run political ads. It would be against these media moguls' interests to support refroming a system that lines their corporate purse. The owners of the Big Five (Disney; Westinghouse; GE; Murdoch's News Corporation, Inc.; and Time-Warner) are themselves major campaign contributors and corrupters of the current system, funnelling millions into the soft money accounts of the Republican and Democratic parties. The returns on their investment are billions in tax breaks, direct subsidies, and other government "thank yous."

My home state of New Hampshire, which hosts the first-in-the-nation presidential primary, celebrates a retail approach to politics where candidates win support at family dinners and coffee klatches. But even home-spun New Hampshire is not immune to the broadcast gag rule on campaign finance reform. When magazine magnate Steve Forbes ran for president in 1996, he made a formidable showing in New Hampshire. Forbes's sales agent was the only network affiliate in the state, ABC's WMUR in Manchester, which received over $600,000 from Forbes in the months prior to the February primary and reported Forbes's comings and goings like personal infomercials. Altogether the presidential candidates pur-chased $2.2 million in political advertising for one broad-cast station that dominates the New Hampshire market, an amount which exposes the myth surrounding the inti-macy of the New Hampshire primary. Television is the main messenger of politics these days and it's not telling the whole story.

A civilian-based diplomacy supports noncommer-cial, nonprofit, and publicly-subsidized media to coun-teract the corporate-controlled, for-profit, private media that dominate political discourse; and works to place media control, ownership, and lobbying at the center of public policy debate. Democracy cannot function or sur-vive without a sufficient medium by which citizens remain informed and engaged in public policy debates.

YOUR TURN: GETTING INVOLVED

What all of us have witnessed over the last two decades is a growing concentration of power and wealth in fewer hands. Non-commercialized space for public gathering is shrinking, while public participation in politics is being handed over to private wealth. This private wealth is in turn dominating our public welfare, our public lands, our public airwaves, our pension trusts, all of which are legally owned by the people, but not controlled by them. This is not democracy. This is a plutocracy, where debate is defined by narrow margins that leave certain longheld assumptions about foreign policy and democracy unchallenged. If we the people remain spectators or a "bewildered herd" we can expect a continuation of corporate-state collusion.

A true democracy requires struggle for economic and social justice in citizen initiatives. It is my hope that progressive organizations will move beyond single-issue priorities, turf wars, or internal struggles to build one strong and united *movement* that casts a wide social safety net to stop our political and economic decline and realize a global civic society that values genuine democracy.

Nancy Snow is Assistant Professor of Political Science at New England College in Henniker, New Hampshire. She is Executive Director of Common Cause/New Hampshire and serves on the Board of Directors of the Cultural Environment Movement (CEM). She thanks Herbert Schiller, Michael Parenti, Robert Klose, and Nancy Harvey for their comments on earlier drafts.

NOTES

1 The Smith-Mundt Act of 1948 (Public Law 402), established the first peace-time propaganda program which led to the creation of the U.S. Information Agency in 1953. Though the objectives of Smith-Mundt were to "promote a better understanding of the U.S. in other countries, and to increase mutual understanding between the people of the United States and the people of other countries," it prohibits the domestic dissemination of any USIA materials produced for overseas information programs.

2 The stated goal of the Fulbright international educational exchange program is to foster mutual understanding and cooperation and is not designed for one-way propagandistic purposes. See the Fulbright-Hays Act (Mutual Educational and Cultural Exchange Act of 1961).

3 For a short discussion of the nature of propaganda, see "What is Propaganda, Anyway?" in *Propaganda Review*, Number 5, Summer 1989. For an extensive discussion, see Harold D. Lasswell, Daniel Lerner, and Hans Speier, Editors, *Propaganda and Communication in World History*, Volumes 1-3. (Honolulu, HI: University of Hawaii Press, 1979/80).

4 Lawrence Ziring, Jack C. Plano, and Roy Olton, *International Relations: A Political Dictionary*, 5th Edition (Denver, CO:ABC-CLIO, 1995).

5 America's propaganda mission is contrasted with Soviet propaganda in books with telling titles: See Edward W. Barrett, *Truth is Our Weapon* (New York: Funk and Wagnall, 1953); Oren Stephens, *Facts to a Candid World* (Stanford: Stanford University Press, 1955); Wilson P. Dizard, *The Strategy of Truth: The Story of the U.S. Information Service* (Washington: Public Affairs Press, 1961); and Joshua Muravchik, *Exporting Democracy: Fulfilling America's Destiny* (Washington, AEI Press, 1991).

6 Woodrow Wilson, *Message to Congress*, 63rd Congress, 2nd Session, Senate Document No. 566 (Washington, 1914), pp. 3-4.

7 Philip M. Taylor, *Munitions of the Mind* (Manchester, England: Manchester University Press, 1995), p. 178.

8 Woodrow Wilson, *War Message*, 65th Congress, 1st Session, Senate Document No. 5, Serial No. 7264 (Washington, 1917), pp. 3-8.

9 Taylor, p. 183.

10 George Creel, *How We Advertised America: The First Telling of the Amazing Story of the Committee on Public Information That Carried the Gospel of Americanism to Every Corner of the Globe* (New York: Harper & Brothers, 1920).

11 Ibid., p. 7.

12 As quoted in Fitzhugh Green, *American Propaganda Abroad* (New York: Hippocrene Books, 1988), p. 14.

13 Ibid., p. 12.

14 Edward L. Bernays, *Propaganda* (New York: H. Liveright, 1928).

15 See John C. Stauber and Sheldon Rampton, *Toxic Sludge is Good for You:*

Lies, Damn Lies, and the Public Relations Industry (Monroe, ME: Common Courage Press, 1995).

16 Johan Carlisle, "Public Relationships: Hill & Knowlton, Robert Gray, and the CIA," *CovertAction Quarterly*, Number 44, Spring 1993, p. 22.

17 Noam Chomsky, "Market Democracy in a Neoliberal Order: Doctrines and Reality," Davie Lecture, University of Cape Town, South Africa, May 1997.

18 See Mark Dowie's Introduction in *Toxic Sludge is Good For You.*

19 The United States Information and Educational Exchange Act, better known as the Smith-Mundt Act, has been the legislative charter for U.S. overseas information and cultural programs since 1948. (Public Law 80-402)

20 As told to Fitzhugh Green, *American Propaganda Abroad* , p. 26.

21 Thirteenth Report of the United States Advisory Commission on Information, January 1958, p. 9.

22 Everett M. Rogers, *A History of Communication Study: A Biographical Approach* (New York: The Free Press, 1997), p. 214.

23 My former employer, Delphi International, is a private, nonprofit organization which carries out a broad range of educational and training programs. Delphi is one of the U.S. Information Agency's largest implementors of the International Visitor Program.

24 The Mutual Educational and Cultural Exchange Ace, better known as the Fulbright-Hays Act, was signed into law by President John F. Kennedy on September 21, 1961. Public Law 87-256 is still the basic legislative authority for Fulbright and other U.S. government exchange programs administered by the USIA.

25 J. William Fulbright and Seth P. Tillman, *The Price of Empire* (New York: Pantheon Books, 1989).

26 David Clark Scott, "U.S., Canada, Mexico Build University Ties," *Christian Science Monitor*, October 6, 1993, p. 14.

27 Ibid.

28 "USIA Fact Sheet," February 1994.

29 Jeffrey Gayner, "The Fulbright Program After 50 Years: From Mutual Understanding to Mutual Support." (Washington, DC: Capital Research Center, 1995), pp. 13-14.

30 Ibid.

31 "U.S., Mexico, Announce Major Expansion of Fulbright Program," *USIS Washington File*, May 6, 1997.

32 William Drozdiak, "America Accused of Bullying World: Even Allies Resent U.S. Dominance," *Washington Post*, November 4, 1997, p. A1.

33 Klaus Kinkel, quoted in Drozdiak, "Even Allies Resent U.S. Dominance," *The Washington Post*, November 4, 1997.

34 Lionel Jospin, quoted in Drozdiak.

35 Nelson Mandela, quoted in Drozdiak.

36 J. William Fulbright, *The Arrogance of Power* (New York: Vintage Books, 1966), p. 25.

37 Alexis de Tocqueville, quoted in Fulbright, *The Arrogance of Power*, p. 28.

38 Ibid., p. 28.

39 The I-Bureau mission statements are quoted in Ed Taishoff, "The I Bureau: A New Beginning," *USIA World*, Volume 13, Number 5, 1994, p.4.

40 In 1996 I coordinated a program, "The Spin Cycle: Press, Politics, and the New Hampshire Primary," at New England College for a USIA-sponsored group of journalists from 20 countries. One of the accompanying State Department escorts told the Inn proprietor hosting the journalists that some of them were chosen for their strong negative attitudes toward the United States.

41 See Noam Chomsky, "Propaganda, American-style," based on an article in *Propaganda Review* (Winter, 1987/88), interviews conducted by David Barsamian of KGNU in Boulder, Colorado, and a Chomsky essay in *Radical Priorities*, C.P. Otero, editor (Montreal: Black Rose Books, 1984).

42 Walter Lippman, *The Phantom Public* (New York: Harcourt, Brace and Company, 1925).

43 As reported in *Broadcasting and Cable* magazine, March 21, 1994, p. 61.

44 Wayne S. Smith, "Pirating Radio Martí," *The Nation*, January 27, 1997. See also Peter Kornbluh and Jon Elliston, "Pricey, Stupid, and Wrong: Will Congress Kill TV Martí?," *The Nation*, August 22/29, 1994.

45 Pat M. Holt, "Foreign Affairs Budget Gets Nickeled-And-Dimed," *Christian Science Monitor*, March 6, 1997, p. 19.

46 Rushworth M. Kidder, "Project Democracy: Reagan tries to export the U.S. way of governing," *Christian Science Monitor*, March 16, 1983, p. 3.

47 Ibid.

48 Ibid.

49 Anthony Lake, "The Four Pillars to Emerging `Strategy of Enlargement,'" *Christian Science Monitor*, September 29, 1993.

50 Joseph Duffey, Remarks to Senate Foreign Relations Subcommittee on Terrorism, Narcotics, and International Operations, June 17, 1993.

51 Howell Heflin, "Telling America's Story to the World Still Vital Service," USIA editorial, July 5, 1996.

52 Rhonda E. Boris, "Reinventing BNC's and USIS American Centers: Venues for Public Diplomacy and Trade Promotion in the Information Age," *News and Views*, American Federation of Government Employees, Local 1812, May 1994, p. 3.

53 Ibid.

54 Jeff Gerth and Tim Weiner, "Arms Makers See Bonanza in Selling NATO Expansion," *New York Times*, June 27, 1997, p. 1. See also "NATO Rearms the World," *In These Times editorial*, July 28, 1997, p. 2.

55 A 1960s study of the Inter-American system and U.S. political intervention in Latin America concluded that while the U.S. pays lip service to democracy the real objective is "private, capitalist enterprise." See Gordon Connell-Smith, *The Inter-American System* (London: Oxford University Press and Royal Institute of International Affairs, 1966).

56 Joseph Duffey, "A Message from the Director to all USIA Employees," September 4, 1997, outlines Agency vital goals.

57 "A National Security Strategy for a New Century," White House, Executive Office of the President, National Security Council, May 1997, p. 2.

58 Jimmy Carter, Memorandum for Director, International Communication Agency, The White House, March 13, 1978.

59 Fitzhugh Green, *American Propaganda Abroad*, p. 42.

60 Julia Malone, "US Agency Readies New War of Words," *Christian Science Monitor*, October 7, 1981, p. 6.

61 USIA has undergone downsizing cuts under the Clinton Administration. Educational exchanges, including the Fulbright program, have taken 20 percent budget cuts in recent years.

62 The alleged blacklist included David Brinkley, Walter Cronkite, Coretta Scott King, and Ralph Nader.

63 Henry Catto, Address to the National Endowment for Democracy, June 5, 1992.

64 Jim Fuller, "Officials Hail Business Growth in the Soviet Union," USIS Washington File, October 18, 1993.

65 Kenneth J. Cooper, "USIA Hosts Deal-Making Conference for U.S. and South African Firms," *Washington Post*, June 6, 1994.

66 Charles W. Corey, "Africa: One of the `Last Frontiers' for Business," USIS Washington File, May 8, 1997.

67 Jeff Faux, "The American Model Exposed," *The Nation*, October 27, 1997, p. 18.

68 Bruce Wharton and Robert Earle, "USIA and NAFTA: Building a Foundation for Success," United States Information Agency, 1994, p. 3.

69 Six of then-President Salinas' Cabinet in 1994, out of a total of twenty-one, studied in the U.S. One Cabinet member was a Fulbright grantee, four of his sub-Cabinet members had Fulbright grants, and Mexico's top three NAFTA negotiators, Herminio Blanco, Jaime Zabludowsky, and Aslan Cohen were Fulbright grantees.

70 The Coca-Cola Company initially donated $250,000 to be administered by the U.S.-Mexico Fulbright Commission to sponsor environmental study and research. Coca-Cola has also sponsored Fulbright grantees to Venezuela and Germany, and provides the $50,000 remuneration that accompanies the annual J. William Fulbright Prize for International Understanding.

71 Wharton and Earle, p. 4.

72 Ibid., p. 4.

73 For a discussion of the U.S. stranglehold on Canadian culture, see Carl Wilson, "Northern Exposure: Canada Fights Cultural Dumping," *The Nation*, May 20, 1996, pp. 15-18.

74 Wharton and Earle, p. 5.

75 Ibid., p. 7.

76 The Liberal Party of Canada released a detailed plan of its party platform in 1993 entitled, *Creating Opportunity: The Liberal Plan for Canada*, also known as the "Red Book," from which this quote is taken.

77 Mel Clark, "An Open Letter to the Prime Minister: Canadian Culture is not protected under NAFTA," The Canadian Centre for Policy Alternatives, *Monitor*, September 1996.

78 "Change the Culture of the Federal Agencies." (Washington, DC: The Bureau of National Affairs, Inc., Daily Report for Executives, October 9, 1992). This online supplement, circulated throughout USIA, excerpted findings from the Center for Strategic and International Studies (CSIS) in its report, "Strengthening of America Commission First Report."

79 Kim I. Eisler, "Top Lobbyists," *Washingtonian* , January 1998, pp. 170-171.

80 Margaret Ebrahim, Josh Zivo Feit, and Robert Schlesinger, "Under the Influence: The 1996 Presidential Candidates and Their Campaign Advisers." (Washington, DC: Center for Public Integrity, 1996).

81 Carl Jensen, *Censored: The News That Didn't Make the News and Why* (New York: Seven Stories Press, 1995).

82 See Sarah Anderson and Kristyne Peter, "NAFTA's Corporate Con Artists," *CovertAction Quarterly*, Fall 1995; and Esther Schrader, "A Giant Spraying Sound," *Mother Jones*, Jan/Feb. 1995.

83 USA·NAFTA set up a war room operation by enlisting the help of 50 corporate "captains" like AT&T, Zerox, and Allied Signal to garner support in each of the 50 states, backed up by a "force" of 2,000 smaller corporations.

84 David Bonior, "I Told You So," *New York Times*, July 13, 1997, p. 17.

85 "Fast-Track Backtrack," *The Nation* editorial, December 1, 1997.

86 David Crane, "U.S. Circles the Wagons," *The Toronto Star*, November 13, 1997.

87 Thomas Friedman, "U.S. Vision of Foreign Policy Reversed," *New York Times*, September 22, 1993.

88 "Fact Sheet: Foreign Policy Agencies Reorganization," The White House, Office of the Press Secretary, April 18, 1997.

89 "Building Democracy, Open Markets to Remain Administration Goals," USIA Wireless File, December 10, 1996.

90 "Daley Leading Business Group to South America," USIA Wireless File, May 9, 1997.

91 "Brown Viewed Trade as Bolstering Human Rights and Welfare," USIA Wireless File, April 4, 1996.

92 "A Message from the Director to all USIA Employees," September 4, 1997.

93 See my chapter, "The Crisis in Mobility," in *Invisible Crises*, George Gerbner, Hamid Mowlana, and Herbert Schiller, Editors. (Boulder, CO: Westview Press, 1996); and Jerry Mander, "The Dark Side of Globalization," *The Nation*, July 15, 1996.

94 See "Cold War Institutional Relics," in The Cato Handbook for Congress

(Washington, DC: Cato Institute, 1995), pp. 307-312; and Charles A. Schmitz, "Changing the Way We Do Business in International Relations," Cato Policy Analysis No. 245, November 8, 1995.

95 Alan Eisner, "Business Outspent Labor 11-1 in 1996," Reuters News Service, November 25, 1997.

96 Ruth Marcus and John Yang, "Business Leaders Want Bucks to Buck Labor's Ad Campaign," *Washington Post*, November 23, 1997, p. A6.

97 Del Jones, "Wal-Mart tops GM as largest U.S. Employer," *USA Today*, April 9, 1997.

98 The major broadcast networks have corporate parents. Disney owns ABC, Time Warner controls CNN, Fox is owned by Rupert Murdoch's News Corporation, Inc., General Electric owns NBC, and Westinghouse owns CBS. The latter two corporations, GE and Westinghouse, are major U.S. military conglomerates.

99 Jefferson and Dewey quotations are from Noam Chomsky's foreword, "Debunking the Corporate Agenda," in Kevin Danaher, *Corporations Are Gonna Get Your Mama: Globalization and the Downsizing of the American Dream* (Monroe, Maine: Common Courage Press, 1996), pp. 9-10.

100 Ben Bagdikian, *The Media Monopoly*, 5th Edition (Boston: Beacon Press, 1997).

101 For further discussion, see "Introduction: A Second Chance" in Tom Barry and Martha Honey, editors, *Global Focus: A New Foreign Policy Agenda 1997-1998* (Silver City, NM: Interhemispheric Resource Center Press, 1997).

102 "Foes of Land Mines Win Nobel Peace Prize," *International Herald Tribune*, October 11, 1997.

103 Clinton Doesn't Call Nobel Winner," *Associated Press*, October 12, 1997.